D1279730

What people are saying about …

STALLED

"Ministry is challenging. If you're grieving because of loss of a dream, discouraged because of comparison, dissatisfied because of your current situation, it's easy to become isolated and depressed. Dale Sellers brings encouragement, insight, and hope to the pastor who's stalled by delivering biblical wisdom, pastoral empathy, and clear-cut leadership to the real-life trenches of ministry. Read this book! Get one for 'that' friend! Don't go through this alone!"

David Chrzan, pastor, Saddleback Church

"Dale Sellers tells how his desire for success stalled his life and ministry. He was trying to get another leader's results and was not leading the way God made him. Every fulfilled and effective spiritual leader I know has to work through this leadership developmental challenge. I am grateful we have Dale's road map to help us through to the faithfulness, freedom, and fruitfulness on the other side."

Haydn Shaw, author of *Sticking Points and Generational IQ*

"Discouraged. It's how every leader has felt at one point or another when we want to be somewhere we're not. Dale navigated his own experiences of disappointment in himself and uncovered key truths about leadership in ministry that can anchor and guide us today."

Carey Nieuwhof, bestselling author, podcaster, speaker

"This is a great leaders' handbook that you could refer to over and over again. With practical and spiritual principles to apply to your everyday life, Dale offers truths on how not to get caught in the trappings of the enemy and how to propel yourself to the success the Lord has sovereignly planned for your life. A must-read for every church leader!"

Kimberly Boschman, executive director of
Gateway Resource Library, Gateway Church

"If you had an idea about where you thought you'd be in ministry by now, only to have fallen woefully short of that goal, *Stalled* is for you. No, it's not about breaking growth barriers. It's about helping you see the value of where God has placed you so you can become effective and content there.

Karl Vaters, pastor, author of *The Grasshopper Myth, Small Church Essentials* and *100 Days to a Healthier Church*

"Dale Sellers reminds us that God's measuring stick for success in ministry may look very different than ours. Dale's honesty and insight are like medicine for the weary soul. This book will be a great help to those who are searching to keep fighting the good fight of faith and ministry."

Russ Lee, speaker, singer, songwriter, lead singer of NewSong

"As leaders, we have a God-given ambition to make a difference. But for many, life and ministry haven't turned out like we dreamed. This powerful book could be a breakthrough moment for you. With a blend of personal and practical, Dale Sellers will help you walk in freedom and joy in the 'here,' rather than always chasing the illusive 'there.'"

Lance Witt, founder of Replenish Ministries

"Reading this book is like sitting down with a friend who understands what you're feeling. Yet Dale doesn't leave you there; he powerfully helps you move from where you are to where you need to be with a renewed sense of passion and purpose. You need to read this book, and your church needs you to read it too."

Jill and Mark Savage, church planters, speakers, authors of *No More Perfect Marriages*

"Dale has definitively engaged the very struggle that many church leaders everywhere are facing. *Stalled* gives us hope that our struggles and wounds do not have to determine the value of who we are in Christ or the worth of the work God has given us. Whether your ministry is successful or you are flailing to get your church unstuck, this book should definitely be in the hands of every pastor."

Brent J. Carter, director of business development at Faithlife Corp., makers of Logos Bible Software

"I tell leaders all the time: 'Health comes before growth.' Dale has offered a pathway in this book to the health and transformation of the pastor … and then his church! Pastor, grab this book, not to transform your church, but to transform yourself."

Shawn Lovejoy, founder and CEO, CourageToLead.com

"I have had the privilege of a front-row seat to seeing my friend navigate the challenging times with great integrity and then pursue his calling with great diligence. God has uniquely positioned Dale to breathe life into everyone who reads this book!"

Shane Duffey, lead pastor, NewSpring Church

"When you read this book, be prepared to have your soul exposed. More importantly, prepare yourself for the grace of God to bring healing."

Danny Davis, EdD, author of Rural Church Turnaround

"I have a higher level of respect and trust for leaders who have endured and led through tough times. Dale's one of them. Get ready. Dale doesn't hold back. You will be encouraged."

Kem Meyer, communications advocate and author of *Less Chaos. Less Noise.*

"*Stalled* is not your standard platitude-filled 'how to' book. Steering clear of even the hint of condescension, Sellers offers something richer: deep-tissue hope and encouragement."

Mark Rutland, executive director, National Institute of Christian Leadership, author of *Relaunch*

STALLED

Hope and Help for Pastors Who
Thought They'd Be There by Now

DALE SELLERS

DAVID **C** COOK

transforming lives together

STALLED
Published by David C Cook
4050 Lee Vance Drive
Colorado Springs, CO 80918 U.S.A.

Integrity Music Limited, a Division of David C Cook
Brighton, East Sussex BN1 2RE, England

The graphic circle C logo is a registered trademark of David C Cook.

All rights reserved. Except for brief excerpts for review purposes,
no part of this book may be reproduced or used in any form
without written permission from the publisher.

The website addresses recommended throughout this book are offered as a
resource to you. These websites are not intended in any way to be or imply an
endorsement on the part of David C Cook, nor do we vouch for their content.

Unless otherwise noted, all Scripture quotations are taken from THE MESSAGE.
Copyright © by Eugene H. Peterson 1993, 2002. Used by permission of NavPress.
All rights reserved. Represented by Tyndale House Publishers, Inc. Scripture
quotations marked NCV are taken from the New Century Version®. Copyright
© 2005 by Thomas Nelson. Used by permission. All rights reserved; NIV are
taken from THE HOLY BIBLE, NEW INTERNATIONAL VERSION®, NIV®
Copyright © 1973, 1978, 1984, 2011 by Biblica, Inc.® Used by permission. All
rights reserved worldwide; NKJV are taken from the New King James Version®.
Copyright © 1982 by Thomas Nelson. Used by permission. All rights reserved.

Library of Congress Control Number 2020935431
ISBN 978-0-8307-8063-1
eISBN 978-0-8307-8067-9

© 2020 Dale Sellers

The Team: Michael Covington, Alice Crider, Judy Gillispie,
Kayla Fenstermaker, Jon Middel, Susan Murdock
Cover Design: Jon Middel

Printed in the United States of America
First Edition 2020

1 2 3 4 5 6 7 8 9 10

052720

This book is dedicated to all the pastors who thought they'd be there by now. Through these pages, may you receive a renewed sense of purpose and rekindled passion to change the world around you.

CONTENTS

FOREWORD

I agree with Dale. I also thought I'd be there by now.

Because of that, you may just want to skip this foreword. In fact, odds are pretty good that you will skip it. That's what I do when I read a book. I skip over the foreword because I want to get there faster—to the end of the book, that is. (My apologies to the people who have written forewords to my books.)

That penchant for skipping things and wanting to be there faster, though, is the main reason why I thought it might be helpful for you to get a glimpse of my journey.

Before I do that, let me tell you a little bit about here. Today I'm the lead strategist at the Unstuck Group. We help churches get unstuck. I never thought I'd be here.

The reason I say that is because I never planned to launch a ministry that would help hundreds of churches across the world experience health and growth. That's not a brag. It's just an honest admission. It wasn't my dream when I was growing up. It wasn't on my radar when I was going through school. It wasn't my plan when I started my career.

But as it turns out, that's one of the key things I've learned about getting there ... wherever there is. It's less about what I'm doing and more about who I'm becoming. It's less about where I'm located and more about those I'm sharing my life with. It's less about my plans and more about God's purpose.

Before I tell you how to get from here to there, let me share how I arrived here.

My first job (besides mowing lawns) was working in a print shop, helping to prepare orders and assist with delivery. All I can remember is that I despised the collating machine.

Then I took a promotion with Sears. Remember Sears? I sold men's clothing. It's hilarious to think I used to measure old men for polyester suits.

During the two summers following my high school graduation, I worked on the local golf course. My job included mowing greens, cutting new cups, and lots of weed eating.

While I was in college getting my business degree, I commuted about ninety minutes between school and home to be the program manager of a litter prevention and recycling program for the City of Piqua, Ohio. I was the "Litter Czar."

For a couple of years while I was wrapping up my undergraduate degree and getting my graduate degree, I worked as an intern in the city manager's office for the City of Northwood, Ohio.

After graduating from Bowling Green State University (Go Falcons!), I took a job as an assistant in the city manager's office in Galesburg, Illinois. I was primarily responsible for human resources functions, including facilitation of labor negotiations with four different unions.

My first job as a city manager was in Knoxville, Iowa. I was only twenty-five at the time. It's really pretty crazy when you think about it. At that age, I was responsible for leading the departments of police, fire, streets, parks, finance, and so on. Now you know why I'm so committed to raising up and empowering young leaders.

After spending a few years in Iowa, my wife and I moved to Niles, Michigan. The City of Niles hired me to lead a staff team of about a hundred and fifty people and manage about a $20 million budget. That was a lot of money more than twenty years ago. That move also led us to Granger Community Church near South Bend, Indiana.

Later that same year, I responded to a job ad at Granger Community Church for an office manager position. Eventually I was hired to be a pastor at the church. I took a huge pay cut. I also gave up the car allowance and the country club golf membership.

I worked at Granger Community Church for over eight years before moving to NewSpring Church in Anderson, South Carolina, where, among other things, I had the opportunity to help the church launch their multisite strategy.

After my experience at NewSpring, I started the Unstuck Group. Last year, we had the opportunity to serve 125 churches in the United States and Canada.

All that to say, it took about twelve years in various marketplace roles before God transitioned me into ministry. And it's taken me more than twenty years in ministry to get to the place I am today.

Why am I sharing this? I share it for a couple of reasons. First, it's just important to remember that I wouldn't be here today if it weren't for all those *there*s I experienced along the way. Back in the mideighties, while I was operating that collating machine, I could not have done what I'm doing now. And while I am writing this foreword, which you might not read, I may not be prepared for what God has in store for my future.

I say this because the odds are pretty good that God still has more in store for my life. I have a sense of what my future may hold but, based on my journey so far, God's plans might be quite different. He has this way of doing immeasurably more than all I ask or imagine.

Life is a series of next steps. We need to be faithful and disciplined about whatever next step God has for our lives. If we do that, then years from now we'll be able to look back and celebrate what God accomplished in us and through us. It all begins, though, with remaining faithful and diligent where God has us today.

What does God want you to do in this moment? Do that.

Who is it God wants you to learn from right now? Soak in their wisdom.

Why is God allowing you to experience the challenges you face? Lean in. This is part of your journey.

Who is it God has in your life right now? They are in your life for a reason.

You're going to love this book. Dale is not only a good friend; he's a partner in ministry. He loves Jesus, and he loves the churches he serves.

And beyond that, I trust him. He's a man of integrity. The wisdom he shares is essential for pastors in their leadership. More importantly, though, his stories and experiences will reshape your view of your life. Your purpose. Your calling.

When you're finished reading, maybe you'll realize what I did. I need to live today as if I'm already there. This is the life Jesus promised—a rich and satisfying life.

That's how we get from here to there.

Tony Morgan
Founder and Lead Strategist of The Unstuck Group

INTRODUCTION

A disturbing trend has developed in American culture in recent years. Churches are closing by the thousands.[1] Although a definitive number is hard to verify, you've probably seen the effect of this trend in your community too. It's even possible that you have been affected by it personally. It would not be overtly alarmist to conclude that the long-term results of this trend will have far-reaching consequences both now and in future generations if it's not corrected. No group is immune from its impact. I've seen this firsthand as I have worked with many denominations in various geographical regions across the country. And that's not all.

Communities in both rural and urban settings are seeing former church buildings sold or abandoned to become breweries, restaurants, exercise facilities, and nightclubs. There has been a shift in our culture to embrace the vintage architecture of older church designs. It is considered cool to renovate a former sanctuary, because it offers a super nice vibe.

Are you aware that 95 percent of American congregations average fewer than five hundred people in attendance each week, according to the Hartford Institute for Religion Research?[2] In fact, 87 percent of them average fewer than two hundred fifty in attendance.[3] These numbers show that small and midsize churches are the backbone of the American church. The notoriety of many megachurches can lead us to believe they are more numerous than they actually are. This mistaken assumption is due mostly to the broader visual platform and reach they have each week. Yet, in reality, they make up fewer than 5 percent of all churches.

Please know I'm not a megachurch hater. I love the church as a whole. And I'm very thankful for every church that is preaching the gospel, advancing the kingdom, and impacting communities. There is never a good time to hate our fellow believers just because they are different from us.

It was out of love for the church that 95Network was launched. We believe that small and midsize churches are vital in impacting our world for Jesus. However, the majority of the great resources developed to aid in healthy growth are often out of reach for the average church. At 95Network, our mission is to provide big resources to small and midsize churches. And our vision is to bring positive change to every small and midsize church. Simply put, we love helping churches.

THE CHURCH IS THE INSTRUMENT CHOSEN BY GOD TO

ADVANCE HIS KINGDOM.

95Network carries out our mission and vision through what we call the four Cs: content, conferences, coaching, and consulting. Each of the four Cs is designed to provide proven principles and practices that help churches experience healthy growth. You can dive deeper into who we are by going to www.95Network.org.

Before I became the executive director of 95Network, I realized that a deeply held belief had kept me in bondage for most of my ministry. As a small-church pastor, I observed the success of others, and I became so discouraged that I believed my life was a failure because of my inability to get *there*, wherever *there* was. Three decades of faithfully serving in ministry had produced deep-seated self-doubt that affected every area of my life.

The defeated view I had internalized about myself showed up in obvious factors such as comparison, embarrassment, and disappointment.

However, each of these was a symptom rather than the real problem. They served only as daily reminders that I wasn't close to getting *there*.

If you're the pastor or another leader of a small church, perhaps you can relate. The good news is I broke free from the bondage of that discouragement, and so can you.

Back then, my typical daily prayer routine included something like, "Jesus, please don't come back until I fulfill my purpose." Or "Jesus, please don't let me die until I fulfill my purpose."

I was continually worried that He would be disappointed with me when I finally saw Him face to face. I wanted so desperately to hear Him say, "Well done, good and faithful servant" (Matt. 25:23 NKJV). Yet I believed I couldn't do enough to earn those words of affirmation. To be honest, I had no idea what purpose I was trying to fulfill. It always seemed elusive.

The energy I exerted as I ran toward wherever *there* was took a toll on my body. My physical heart issues unveiled the spiritual heart issues, becoming the doorway to much-needed change. I have heard it said that God will allow us to end up on our backs in order to change our focus. This is what happened to me. And I'm eternally grateful.

In the chapters ahead, we'll take a deep dive into the fallacy of believing that our vocational performance somehow determines our value to Jesus. I will show you the specific contributors in my upbringing that led me to live every day in a "stress prison." The majority of these were more *caught* than *taught*.

This book is divided into three sections: "Why Can't I Get There?," "What Will I Find There?," and "The Fulfillment of Living There." The goal of *Stalled* is to help you spend the rest of your days living in the freedom and purpose that Jesus has always intended for you to experience. I want you to discover, as I did, that He has already removed the door from the prison cell that has kept you from getting *there*. The time has arrived for you to walk out of that cell.

My freedom experience was set in motion through the words of a dear friend: "You can't let God down because you're not holding Him up." His insight gave me the courage to tell God how I felt about where I had arrived. One morning during prayer, I confessed that I couldn't understand why He wasn't using me to help more people. I had reasoned that He would want to use my life experiences, giftedness, and connections. However, the conversation went in a different direction, and I began to see that I couldn't let God down because He's not counting on me alone to accomplish His purposes. My frustrated confession allowed Him to pry open the tightly shut door in my heart.

That encounter with God provided an opportunity to hear how He felt about me. I discovered He wasn't keeping score. I also began to see that my life could have a lasting impact not by me working *for* Him but by Him working *through* me. How had I missed that truth for more than thirty years?

IT'S TIME TO TURN SELF-DOUBT INTO CONFIDENCE THAT HE WHO STARTED SOMETHING IN YOU IS THE ONE WHO WILL FINISH WHAT HE STARTED.

My ultimate hope in writing *Stalled* is to expose a plan devised by Satan himself to destroy the church of Jesus Christ. It is no secret that on earth the church is the main resistance to the forces of hell. The church is the instrument chosen by God to advance His kingdom, bring spiritually dead people to life, and destroy the works of darkness. If Satan can discourage and disarm church leaders appointed by Jesus, then he can neutralize our impact in our communities and culture. Simply put, a defeated pastor will create a defeated church.

When you're in a raging battle that won't relent, you can become so inward focused that you miss the bigger purpose of the war. While defeating the church of today is always Satan's mission, he is fighting to win a greater war that we can't afford to lose.

If you have arrived at the same point of discouragement in your ministry, *Stalled* will provide some solid solutions. I want you to discover that what you've been looking for out *there* has actually been with you the whole time. It's time to turn self-doubt into confidence that He who started something in you is the One who will finish what He started (Phil. 1:6). No matter the size of your ministry or organization, you are a vital part of advancing the kingdom today and ensuring its success for generations to come.

Somebody has got to help turn the tide of this negative trend. Our world can't afford to have people eating burgers and pizza in buildings that were designed to feed them the Bread of Life. If you too have thought you would *be there by now*, then join me on a journey to the freedom that comes from partnering *with* Him rather than working *for* Him.

WHY CAN'T I GET THERE?

THE LOOK OF THE PAST

In 1989 the rock band Queen released a song titled "I Want It All." The chorus blares, "I want it all, and I want it now."[4]

In many ways, "I Want It All" describes the mindset that prevailed in the United States throughout the 1980s. And if we're honest with one another, we still have the same mindset. So whether you grew up rocking out or not, I imagine you probably have to deal with being impatient at times. I know I do.

I mention this up front because there's a good chance you picked up this book to discover why you've become stalled and how to move forward. And you probably want the answers now. I get that.

In our instant drive-through culture, we've become accustomed to quick fixes and immediate results. Every arena of life pressures us to turn things around quickly. A great example of this is found in sports. Seldom are fan bases and large donors patient enough to allow a new head coach and his or her staff enough time to build a winning culture. Winning now is more important than structuring for long-term success. Therefore, it has become common for coaches to be fired within two years if they haven't won a championship.

Sadly, this mindset prevails in so many of our churches as well. A church hires a new leader, expecting that person to draw new families. When this doesn't happen fast enough, the church starts looking for someone else who can get things going in the right direction. The underlying hope for many congregations is to somehow find the magic bullet of success.

There's a high possibility that you have fallen into this trap if you are a stalled leader. Maybe you are frantically searching for the right conference, the hottest podcast, or a bestselling book that will reveal what you need to do to get *there* quickly. If so, you need to know that the magic bullet of success doesn't exist. However, there is an immediate action you can take if you're ready to get things rolling in the right direction again.

I started moving in the right direction when I finally told someone how I honestly felt. Confessing to a friend that I felt like a failure began the process of change for me. It obviously didn't solve all my problems in that moment. But allowing myself to open up to someone did put me on a course toward healing.

Take a moment now and identify someone you trust that you can tell how you're feeling about where you are today. Let that person know you are working through a book designed to help you move in a positive direction. Then, keep him or her abreast of your progress. (Maybe even ask this person to read it as well in order to hold you accountable.)

Accountability to a trusted friend will be vital in helping you get *there*. Questions have been included at the end of each chapter for reflection. You will benefit from going over these questions with your confidant.

Just in case you need something else to focus on, let me offer you this word of advice that I often share with pastors who reach out to 95Network. I talk weekly with discouraged pastors all across the country. The most important thing I tell them to do immediately is to develop a clearly defined mission. I'm not referring to a well-crafted statement that is several pages long. That's a book, not a mission.

Your mission simply explains why you exist as an organization. It should be stated in about twelve words or less. It clearly communicates to everyone throughout the organization why you believe you are in your community at this particular time in history. Throughout *Stalled*, you will find help in defining your mission. Once you define it, you can proceed with practical and proven steps to structure for sustained and healthy growth.

In the pages ahead, I'll share how I got stalled so you can recognize the challenges of being stalled and embrace the solutions that can move you into fulfilling the mission Jesus created you to carry out. My journey to being *unstalled* began many years ago. Think of me as your guide who went before you.

I grew up around the construction business. Dad was a successful home builder who built hundreds of homes during my childhood. I spent every summer and holiday on the jobsite. My life's goal was to have my own home-building business one day too. Therefore, at eighteen years old, I got my residential builder's license.

As much as I loved working with my hands, I was always fascinated with heavy machinery. It was so cool to watch a bulldozer move dirt around while grading a lot for a new home. I would have become a heavy-machinery operator if I hadn't chosen to become a carpenter.

My fascination with heavy equipment led to one of the worst situations of my life in my midthirties. Our family was in the process of building a log home. When you purchase a log home package, the company sends all the materials to your jobsite on large trucks. The buyer is in charge of securing a forklift in order to unload them. We rented the biggest forklift I have ever seen. The tires were as tall as me. It was awesome. Not wanting to take a chance on causing a delay for the truck drivers, I had the forklift delivered a day early. That was when my situation began.

The temptation to "practice" operating the forklift was more than I could resist. After all, I needed to make sure I understood how it worked. Wouldn't that be the responsible thing to do? So I hopped into the driver's seat and spent the next several hours "practicing." Of course, I was just playing on a big piece of machinery … and, boy, was it fun—until I stalled out in the mud.

In my effort to test how far the boom arm would reach, I didn't notice that I had begun to sink. The more I moved back and forth, the deeper the forklift sank. Finally, it was so deep that the undercarriage was sitting on the ground and all four tires were spinning. The more I tried to get free, the more stalled I became. By then it was six o'clock in the evening, and there were three trucks full of materials scheduled to arrive the next morning at seven. How would we unload them now?

I sat there thinking about the mess I'd gotten myself into. The look on my face said it all. *How could I have been so irresponsible? This is 100 percent my fault.* The pressure continued to build as I realized what I had to do next because there was no other option.

WHEN YOU FIND YOURSELF STALLED OUT, THE BEST THING YOU CAN DO IS REACH OUT FOR HELP.

When you find yourself stalled out, the best thing you can do is reach out for help. I called a friend, who came and pulled me out with his bulldozer. Without question, that was one of the most embarrassing experiences of my life.

The hardest part was having to own up to what led me to become stalled in the first place. I was trying to do something I hadn't been trained to do. I thought I could handle it on my own and just wing it without any supervision. Obviously, my thinking was wrong.

I experienced the same feeling a few months later while I was pastoring a small church. Our little congregation grew from thirty to three hundred. However, it went back down to one hundred fifty because of a nasty church split. That split revealed three key areas of my leadership that had played a part in the problem. I was *unable* because of a lack of training, *unaware* of what was really happening, and *unfulfilled* by what I was accomplishing.

1

UNABLE

*Don't compare your beginning to someone else's middle, or your
middle to someone else's end. Don't compare the start of your
second quarter of life to someone else's third quarter.*

—Tim Hiller, *Strive*

"I thought I'd be there by now," I confessed to my friend Tony Morgan
several minutes into our conversation about leadership issues. I had never
had the courage to express this thought out loud before. But it was true
… wherever *there* was. I felt as though I hadn't accomplished enough.
But after blurting out my thoughts with such gut-level honesty, my life
started to change.

Unintentionally I had subscribed to the false belief that success
was directly related to building something huge and meaningful for the
masses. *Why don't I have a large church yet?* I wondered. *There must be
something wrong with me as a person and a leader.*

Many people from all walks of life begin to sense increasing pressure
as we get older. By then it's clear that life is not going to turn out as we
hoped. It happens in our marriages, our parenting, and our vocations. It
happens with our homes, our travel (or lack thereof), our bank accounts,
and our hobbies. I'm amazed by the number of twenty- and thirtysome-
things I meet who already feel disappointment about not having reached

the milestones they think they should have reached, even with so much life still ahead of them.

THE LOOK

Maybe your current experience in ministry could best be described as *stalled*. Has the stress from thinking you would be there by now caused you to adopt the look of the leader who doesn't know what to do next? Maybe you've tried what the "experts" have offered as guarantees for growth only to discover that you become more stalled with each new attempt to get moving.

In most instances, the pressure we feel is coming from the inside. But we keep pressing on, and the very joy of living gets sucked right out of us. We develop a certain *look* over the years. I see it in people's eyes on a daily basis. I notice it on the faces of people from all age groups, backgrounds, cultures, and walks of life. It is so common for me to see it in the eyes of the pastors I work with across the United States. I imagine you have probably seen it too—maybe when you looked in the mirror this morning.

Sadly, I had this look for most of my life, but I didn't reach out for help. I simply suffered in silence while outwardly maintaining a positive approach to life. Eventually, the weight of it brought about so much stress that I ended up having open-heart surgery. Friend, that is no way to live.

What is the look, and how do we get it?

The look comes from having a sense that we have failed and that failure defines us. It comes from the feeling of being unable to fulfill our calling. It's the undeniable evidence that we thought we'd be there by now. But the real problem is unrealistic expectations and a wrong definition of success.

As you reflect for a moment, are you aware that you have the look? If so, I want to help you by unpacking how we get it—and how we get free from it. I want to take you on a confidence-gaining journey, and my hope is that you will develop a healthy self-image filled with great assurance that you will fulfill your purpose.

The objective is not to create the illusion of confidence. Instead, the goal is to equip you with the tools to define real success, discover the secret of setbacks, and ultimately discern how to become a source of blessing to others.

Admitting I thought I'd be there by now dislodged something that had been holding me back for a long time. It became the defining moment when I began experiencing true freedom. Yes, it was terrifying and embarrassing. But it was also liberating.

Confessing my feelings of failure out loud to Tony caused a breakthrough inside me that felt like a thousand-pound weight lifting off my chest. Simultaneously it became the point at which Jesus began a deep healing process in my heart. Revealing my belief allowed my heart to begin releasing a negative self-image buried deep inside for decades. If the countenance is a mirror of the soul, then there is no doubt that my constant disappointment and self-doubt caused me to develop the look.

I wonder whether you have the look too. Can we be honest with each other? Really honest? How would you respond if we were having coffee face to face today and I mentioned that you have the look? Would you be embarrassed or defensive? Maybe you would try to steer the conversation in a different direction. You could begin to point out my flaws, of which there are many, by the way. Or you might agree with my assessment but have no real intention of dealing with it.

Acknowledging that we have a problem is the first step to becoming free of it. I'm sure you have probably heard that "the definition of insanity is doing the same thing over and over and expecting different results."[5] The good news is that there is a life of fulfilling ministry available to you on the other side of confronting your disappointment. I know firsthand the freedom that comes through honest confession.

Please don't misunderstand my motive. I'm not judging you. As I have already mentioned, I had that look for most of my ministry life, so I can easily relate to you. That look isn't unique to those in ministry, by the way. In fact, it's on the faces of thousands—maybe millions—of people from all walks of life.

Seasons of setbacks can destroy dreams, cause callousness, burn bridges, harden our hearts, fuel cynicism, and lead to self-doubt. When this happens, we usually build cocoons of protection around ourselves in order to help us hide in plain sight. The cocoons make it possible to carry out our daily responsibilities while our problem goes undetected by those we lead. At least, we hope it does.

A LIFETIME IN THE MAKING

The setting in which I confessed that I thought I'd be there by now was a casual conversation. However, the thought became ingrained in me many years earlier as I was pastoring a small church. I soon learned that each level of growth requires different strategies and structures. That was when I realized that having the leadership ability to reach three hundred people does not automatically mean you have what it takes to reach six hundred or even one thousand. My problem surfaced at some point during that time.

The problem was comparison, and it tormented me. I had allowed myself to view the success of others as a measure of whether I believed I was a success or a failure. In hindsight, it's easy to see where I got offtrack.

ISSUES WE DON'T DEAL WITH DON'T DISSOLVE;

THEY DESTROY.

Comparison, no matter in what arena of life, is always destructive. We see its discouraging effects in such things as how teenage girls relate to one another, the way athletes measure themselves against their competition, the intense stress created by academic achievement, and even our focus on economic status as we try to keep up with the Joneses. It seems all of us are constantly comparing ourselves with … well, everybody else.

Comparison had an even greater negative impact on me because of whom I was comparing myself with. Although our church fit squarely in the 95 percent of all churches, I compared myself with the 5 percent of larger-church pastors. I unintentionally locked myself in a maximum-security prison of comparison as I measured my ministry success against the churches that drew thousands of worshippers each week. No wonder I felt like a failure. Who wouldn't?

By admitting I thought I'd be there by now, I allowed Jesus to unveil the false beliefs behind the shame I had lived under continuously. My shame manifested itself in a sense of failure because the results I had produced in life did not meet the standard I believed He had set for me. It's a hard cross to bear when you believe that Jesus is disappointed with you. Can you relate? Maybe your story is similar. If so, I understand.

I grew up in a traditional church that taught we are saved by grace through faith. However, I observed that most of the people attending our church were often works oriented. To make matters worse, their conversations seemed to say that God was always keeping score of our performance to determine if He was pleased with us.

I would attend youth events where the speaker taught that a big video screen in heaven would show the story of my life to everyone. The video would display my failures for all to see. I was especially troubled to learn that God had called me to reach certain people with the gospel. The big video screen would display everyone in hell that I had failed to reach. It's not hard to understand how I began to think Jesus was disappointed with me when I failed to convert the many lost people I interacted with each day.

At the same time that this performance-based thinking was becoming a part of me, another aspect of my personality was taking shape. I began to notice I had leadership abilities. Peers would often come to me for advice and counsel during high school. Teachers even acknowledged I had the potential to become a person of influence. Although I didn't know it at the time, a perfect storm was brewing that would become the source of tremendous stress in the coming years.

Even though I struggled with making a commitment for a few months, I eventually committed my life to serve in full-time ministry. Attending a Christian college immediately provided an outlet to serve through while I was in school. I toured with a music group from the school, and after graduation, my wife, Gina, and I formed our own music group called Mainstream. The touring experience allowed us to meet hundreds of pastors and church staffers over a ten-year period.

THE CRACKS IN MY LIFE THAT BROUGHT ME SHAME ARE ACTUALLY THE PLACES WHERE HE SHINES THROUGH THE BRIGHTEST.

Like anyone in church leadership, I experienced highs and lows in my formative years of ministry. A pattern emerged that I describe as having the rug pulled out from under me whenever a great opportunity appeared. I often felt that Jesus was dangling a carrot in front of me only to jerk it back because He was disappointed by what my life had produced. I felt deeply unsatisfied at every turn. I didn't know how to define what success looked like in ministry. Even though I couldn't define it, I knew I wasn't achieving it. I just couldn't seem to get there.

Performance-based people like me eventually wear themselves out. Every bad decision I have made throughout my adult life can be attributed to exhaustion. In addition, when I was working with my dad in construction, he would say, "Do something, even if it's wrong." His point was to stay busy and not stand around on the jobsite. Sadly, those words influenced me greatly, and I allowed this thinking to contribute to some bad leadership decisions that resulted in devastating situations.

The most traumatic situation was the church split I mentioned earlier. The first few years of serving as a lead pastor had gone quite smoothly. However, I made some poor decisions that developed out of my unwillingness to deal with my leadership shortcomings. I decided that they would somehow work themselves out if I gave them enough time. But I soon discovered that issues we don't deal with don't dissolve; they destroy.

The ramifications of failed leadership in ministry often can be too difficult to overcome. It had a profound effect on my confidence to lead as well as on my physical well-being. I don't like reliving painful memories, but they are part of my story. I had to come to grips with the fact that I had some wrong views about my relationship with Jesus. I became a Christian at seven years old and had faithfully attended church all my life. But it wasn't until I was stripped of all confidence that God began to do a deep work in me. I now realize I didn't understand what it meant to be in ministry or even what intimacy with Jesus was all about.

The goal of most pastors is the same. We want to hear Jesus say to us, "Well done, good and faithful servant" (Matt. 25:23 NKJV). Yet I felt as if that were no longer an option. In my mind, my performance had produced results of wood, hay, and stubble that would be burned up at the judgment seat of Christ (1 Cor. 3:12–15). He would then begrudgingly allow me to enter heaven by the skin of my teeth to take up residence in the far corners of heaven reserved for those who had wasted their calling. I would probably end up being a street sweeper.

The Bible tells us, "We have this treasure in jars of clay" (2 Cor. 4:7 NIV). I spent a great deal of time while in ministry trying to cover the cracks and scars of my life. However, I am beginning to understand that the cracks in my life that brought me shame are actually the places where He shines through the brightest. Maybe it's time for you to realize that your greatest season of fruitfulness is about to begin as well.

HE MUST FIRST DO A WORK IN HIS PASTORS IN ORDER TO

DO A WORK IN HIS CHURCH.

Friend, are you willing to muster the courage necessary to deal with the source of your problem? I believe we are on the brink of revival that could be the greatest move of God the world has ever experienced. If Jesus is getting His church ready for the great wedding day, doesn't it make sense that He must first do a work in His pastors in order to do a work in His church?

EXPOSED

I remember lying in my bed at night during the season of our church split, wondering if my heart was going to stop because of the stress I was experiencing. This was actually the beginning of some health issues that culminated in quadruple bypass surgery fifteen years later. My heart surgeon considered the stress of ministry to be a major contributor to my condition, which he termed a "widow-maker."

I felt so exposed at the time, as if the whole world could see my leadership shortcomings. I can't stand to be exposed. I know my resistance to exposure is rooted in pride. Maybe some insecurity too. Whatever my real issue is, nothing in life makes me to want to run and hide more. A few times, I wanted to leave town and never go back due to the embarrassment of exposure.

Feelings of inadequacy can wear you down when life doesn't turn out as you hoped. It is obvious when a ministry is stalled. Everyone can see it. Your inability to do anything about the situation eventually causes you to conclude that nothing can be done.

In reality, a lot of us are in the same place. As I mentioned earlier, research continues to reveal that the vast majority of American churches are small. This reality can't be merely coincidental. There must be some common factors that contribute to it.

Here are a few that come to mind:

- the politics of congregational government
- a lack of leadership training
- the widening generational gap
- no clear mission or vision
- programs versus a defined discipleship pathway

Any—or all—of these may be contributing to why your ministry hasn't grown as you had hoped. However, the issue you must confront isn't *how* you arrived at this point. The issue is that you *are* at this point. The lack of growth can't be ignored or explained away. It's just there as a daily reminder that you have been unable to carry out your plans. The results are in at this point, and the picture being painted isn't pretty. So you do your best each day, all the while knowing you are exposed.

Remember my story of being stalled in the mud? The solution came when I reached out for help even though it was the last thing I wanted to do. Honestly, it took a while for me to call my friend. However, the exposure of sitting on a forklift that is going nowhere fast has a way of wearing down your pride. I finally had to admit I was unable to solve my problem on my own.

I also discovered that comparing myself with others when I'm stalled is a waste of time. They can see that I'm stalled. It's embarrassing to try to convince those around me that I'm not stalled while I just sit there. But I resisted making that call with everything in me. Isn't that crazy?

FRIEND, PLEASE STOP GIVING UP ON YOURSELF. DON'T QUIT. I PROMISE THERE IS HOPE, HEALING, AND RESTORATION WAITING FOR YOU.

Thankfully, my pride wore out and my willingness to acknowledge my need for help got me moving again. In so many ways, the same thing happened as I shared my heart with Tony. Healing began to take root in my heart when I accepted that I can't do ministry alone.

Friend, please stop giving up on yourself. Don't quit. I promise there is hope, healing, and restoration waiting for you. The pages ahead are filled with honest examples and proven methods for experiencing a great life after being stalled. Now that you are willing to confront your situation, let's work together to get you moving forward along the path that Jesus has for you. You have so much fruitfulness waiting for you in the days ahead.

DIGGING DEEPER

1. When have you felt exposed in ministry?
2. What results in your ministry so far make you feel unsuccessful?
3. What excuses do you find yourself using for why your church is small?
4. Do you avoid colleagues with larger ministries when you see them? If so, why?

5. Do you feel unsuccessful because you thought surely you would be there by now? Where did you envision being?

If you don't know where to turn or whom to reach out to, please contact 95Network.org and allow us to help. If we don't know the answer to your need, we will do our best to connect you with one of our Strategic Partners who can help.

2

UNAWARE

At best, people are open to scrutinizing themselves and considering
their blind spots; at worst, they become defensive and angry.

—Sheryl Sandberg, *Lean In*

The story of Elijah reveals how he arrived at a place of despair. After running from Jezebel, he prayed, "Enough of this, GOD! Take my life—I'm ready to join my ancestors in the grave!" Then "exhausted, he fell asleep under the lone broom bush" (1 Kings 19:4–5).

Elijah's story has always fascinated me. How could a man of God who had just prayed for fire to fall from heaven get discouraged enough to want to die a few days later? He had seen God do incredible things through him as well as for him ... Now he was deciding to quit? What happened to him?

What happened to Elijah is the same thing that makes all of us think we should be there by now. He got blindsided. The lesson for us is that it doesn't matter whether you can call down fire from heaven or if you're leading a church of thirty. Any leader can be blindsided.

The reason you get blindsided isn't just to stop you from being effective today. It's much more than that. The ultimate purpose is to destroy your ability to be effective in the future. We will dive deeper into this long-term hidden agenda a little later.

MY BLIND SPOT

Several years ago, a group of college students from our church set out from South Carolina on their way to Daytona Beach, Florida, for spring break. They were really pumped up to spend a week "thawing out" on the warm Florida beach after several months of cold weather. They mapped out a path from Clemson University in the Upstate of South Carolina that would take them along Interstate 95 in the eastern part of the state, down through Georgia, and into Florida. Once they crossed the Florida state line, it would only be a matter of a few hours until they arrived in Daytona Beach. Woo-hoo! *Let spring break begin …*

The trip should have taken about eight hours max. However, much to their dismay, it ended up lasting more than fifteen hours. The delay wasn't due to outward circumstances such as road construction, bad weather, or even a horrific traffic accident. Their delay was actually caused by something simple. As they embarked on the journey, they were focused more on *where* they were going than *how* to get there. This minor distraction caused them to head in the wrong direction when starting out. Instead of going south on the interstate, they headed north. Amazingly, no one noticed the mistake until they crossed the North Carolina–Virginia state line. The excited beachgoers had driven over seven hours in the opposite direction of their intended destination.

As leaders, you and I entered ministry with hopes and dreams of making a difference in the lives of many. Our joy was uncontainable. We weren't concerned with accolades and self-promotion. Such thoughts seldom entered our minds. Instead, we set out on this exciting journey of serving Jesus with the goal of advancing the kingdom by growing healthy churches. And if we're honest, even though we knew we would face obstacles, we fully expected to be successful.

So what happened? How did you arrive at this place of discouragement and disillusionment? Is it possible you started out with the best of intentions only to discover you were headed in the wrong direction? Or maybe you honestly have no idea what happened. Many of us understand we have a problem. However, we can't seem to discover what the problem actually is.

I'm sure you have faced some daunting challenges on your leadership journey. They are just part of life. For me, the pressure of challenges is greater when everyone is looking to me for answers, direction, and even comfort. Some of my finest leadership moments have been when I was able to listen to the Holy Spirit and rely on my experience and intuition to navigate difficult circumstances. Few things will create more clout with those we lead than when we come out on the other side victorious.

I have also had several leadership failures when facing challenges. My greatest failures happen when I get blindsided by a problem. It's as if an unseen force launches an assault against me in a battle I didn't even know I was engaged in. I'm unaware of it until something goes wrong. Seldom is there a more difficult situation to overcome than being blindsided. The time needed to assess and react is not available when you feel ambushed. The attack usually ends in defeat.

The precursor to being blindsided is developing blind spots. The biggest problem with my blind spots is that I can't see them, although many of the people around me can easily identify them. I find it fascinating that I can be oblivious to things in my life that are obvious to others. I'm not sure if this happens because I'm unaware of who I really am or because I intentionally ignore the problems.

Both of those reasons for blind spots are detrimental to effective leadership. And intentionally ignoring them comes with an ever-increasing price. There has always been a cost to effective leadership.

I once attended a leadership conference where John Maxwell taught about the accumulating benefits of being able to change as a leader. He compared the ability to change to how compound interest works in a savings account. No matter how much you start out with, the power of compound interest can turn a small investment into a large sum over time. I believe the same principle is often at play when it comes to leadership effectiveness—only in reverse.

Starting out with a leadership deficit is not uncommon or fatal. There are simply some things to learn through experience, whether or not we have previously studied them. However, something happens to us as time goes by if we continue to ignore problems. Uneasiness sets in as the cost of change starts increasing.

FEW THINGS WILL CREATE MORE CLOUT WITH THOSE WE LEAD THAN WHEN WE COME OUT ON THE OTHER SIDE VICTORIOUS.

An unwillingness to change will always work against us. The cost of correcting a character flaw or lack of training is much cheaper in our twenties than in our forties or fifties. Simply put, the reason so many leaders are unwilling to change is that they can no longer afford the price. Or they just refuse to pay it. Either way, interest has compounded against them.

It took some time for me to discover my leadership deficiencies after I entered the ministry. I began to learn that it takes more than preaching and praying to build a healthy ministry. Even if you have an encouragement gift like me, becoming everyone's cheerleader will only take you so far. Eventually, to my dismay, it became apparent that I didn't really know what I was doing. I had read a lot of books on how to be successful. But implementing their advice wasn't giving me any traction.

My fear of being exposed caused me to dig in my heels in order to gain secure footing. I expended a great deal of energy trying to mask my shortcomings and never really reached out for help. Instead of pursuing Jesus, I desperately tried to find what I must be missing. I also spent a lot of time becoming an expert deer hunter as a distraction from ministry. If you allow yourself to follow this path, you will soon discover that you are continually discouraged.

How would you feel to discover that what you thought was holding you back wasn't the problem at all? Would it be a relief to finally know the truth? Or is it possible that you would make the problem worse by refusing to acknowledge it? Even worse, what if you were completely oblivious to the problem? The trouble with blind spots is we don't know what we don't know. But when they are revealed, we can begin to deal with them.

Several years ago, I began to understand my blind spot of measuring my relationship with Jesus from a performance-based, or works-based, point of view. Like most folks, I was apprehensive about dealing with it at first. But acknowledging and working on it took me down a path I wish I would have traveled much earlier. Similar to the students heading to Daytona Beach, I spent many years trying to get free only to discover I was becoming more bound with each passing year—because I was going the wrong direction.

The real issue in those early years was that I was driven to perform in order to earn the Lord's favor. I continuously lived with the concern that He was going to be disappointed with me. Each new day increased my fear that Jesus would be disappointed with the *results* of my ministry life when I finally saw Him in heaven. There would come a day when I would be exposed as having achieved less than He expected of me. The pressure and shame were relentless. And they continued to increase.

The pressure to perform eventually infiltrated every aspect of my life. Even though I knew theologically that my performance didn't bring me closer to God, my internal dysfunction took control of me. I needed to do works for affirmation. Simply put, I needed to show something in order to feel approved. This blind spot became a normal part of my daily routine.

I even had a mental picture of a performance scale that divided life into three categories: my personal spiritual life, my family life, and my professional life. It looked something like this:

DALE'S ANNUAL PERFORMANCE SCALE

1st Quarter:

Category	Personal Life	Family Life	Professional Life
100%	___	___	___
90%	X	___	___
80%		X	
70%	___	___	___
60%	___	___	___
50%	___	___	___
40%	___	___	___
30%	___	___	___
20%	___	___	___
10%	___	___	X
0	___	___	___

2nd Quarter:

Category	Personal Life	Family Life	Professional Life
100%	___	___	___
90%	___	___	___
80%	___	___	___
70%	X	___	___
60%		X	
50%	___	___	___
40%	___	___	X
30%	___	___	___
20%	___	___	___
10%	___	___	___
0	___	___	___

3rd Quarter:

Category	Personal Life	Family Life	Professional Life
100%	___	___	___
90%	___	___	___
80%	___	___	_X_
70%		X	
60%	___	___	___
50%	___	___	___
40%	_X_	___	___
30%	___	___	___
20%	___	___	___
10%	___	___	___
0	___	___	___

4th Quarter:

Category	Personal Life	Family Life	Professional Life
100%	___	___	___
90%		X	
80%	___	___	___
70%	___	___	_X_
60%	___	___	___
50%	___	___	___
40%	___	___	___
30%	___	___	___
20%	_X_	___	___
10%	___	___	___
0	___	___	___

Note the position of my family life on the scale. The horizontal line highlights how I measured everything against our family life. I had made a commitment to my wife and three daughters that I would always choose them over ministry. In looking back on it, I see that the commitment to always put family first was unquestionably the most important absolute I could have established. My family is what kept me from falling apart. Even in the most difficult situations, having a peaceful family life and a wonderful home to return to each day kept me from giving up.

Despite prioritizing family, I eventually wore down. I found myself constantly trying to arrive at a place that always was just out of reach. I can honestly say that I don't remember a season when I allowed myself to score high marks in all three categories. Even if I scored well in two, there was always one category that revealed I had dropped off and needed to improve my performance. No matter what I accomplished, it never seemed to be enough. I couldn't ever be sure if I had done enough to score high marks or earn God's approval. I simply couldn't get *there*.

IT'S TIME TO STOP CARRYING THE WEIGHT OF SHAME

THAT WAS NEVER INTENDED FOR YOU.

How do you keep track of your performance? You probably aren't an obnoxious compulsive like me, but maybe you occasionally feel like success is just out of reach. Or maybe you are a lot like me. Do you feel as if you conclude every evening by reflecting on how you came up short that day? Does feeling like you are somehow disappointing Jesus also weigh heavy on your heart? If you relate to these questions, then you are probably out of balance.

I wonder whether you also have developed the blind spot of shame. Have you resorted to using your own abilities to grow the church, only to find them ineffective? Or have you reached the point where you actually try to hide from Jesus while leading His church? Is the pressure to perform exacting a heavy toll on your life?

Remember, the first step to freedom is admitting you have a problem. It's time to stop carrying the weight of shame that was never intended for you.

SITTING VERSUS SERVING

As they continued their travel, Jesus entered a village. A woman by the name of Martha welcomed him and made him feel quite at home. She had a sister, Mary, who sat before the Master, hanging on every word he said. But Martha was pulled away by all she had to do in the kitchen. Later, she stepped in, interrupting them. "Master, don't you care that my sister has abandoned the kitchen to me? Tell her to lend me a hand."

The Master said, "Martha, dear Martha, you're fussing far too much and getting yourself worked up over nothing. One thing only is essential, and Mary has chosen it—it's the main course, and won't be taken from her." (Luke 10:38–42)

As a pastor, you have probably taught on this passage many times. The normal takeaway is that Martha was the server and Mary was the sitter. However, the story also reveals that Martha sat for a period of time, because it says she "was pulled away by all she had to do in the kitchen." Likewise, it indicates that Mary served, because Martha complained, "My sister has abandoned the kitchen to me." Both women made a choice about how they would respond to Jesus being in the house. I believe they chose based on their natural default.

If I'm being completely transparent, I have a feeling I would have done exactly what Martha did. I would have assumed that my service that day was being rated. I would have expected Jesus to peer through His spiritual microscope and critique my performance. And I would be called out and evaluated in front of everyone at evening's end. Like Martha, I would have been so caught up in serving Jesus that I would have inadvertently ignored simply hanging out with Him. After all, there's so much work to be done in performing for Him. What would you have done in this scenario? What do you still do?

I had never given much thought to Jesus' final comment to Martha. However, there is something in His message to her that really convicts me today. Jesus said, "One thing only is essential, and Mary has chosen it—it's the main course, and won't be taken from her" (Luke 10:42). Only one thing is essential. Just *one*. He defined the one thing by saying Mary chose it. The one thing is to enjoy His presence. That truth is so convicting to me. Jesus even reinforced its importance by saying this one thing wouldn't be taken from her.

CONSISTENT LIFE-CHANGING MINISTRY HAPPENS ONLY WHEN HE SPEAKS HIS HEART TO US IN AN ATMOSPHERE OF INTIMACY.

Let that sink in for a moment. The choice to enjoy His presence will not be taken away. I believe this is why Jesus said it's essential. The scene of this lesson isn't coincidental. Jesus was making a point for all of us who are more driven to serve than to sit. Every one of us has to make a decision as to how we are going to operate in ministry.

We can choose to serve Jesus while ignoring the intimate relational aspects of being His children—a choice that leads us to depend on our own ability. Or we can choose to sit, consistently choosing the atmosphere of His presence that He promised would not be taken away. This choice, by the way, allows Him to carry out His kingdom plan by ministering through us.

This choice to sit doesn't mean you are idle or, God forbid, lazy. It just means you get direction and power in His presence before you attempt to carry out your ministry. To put it another way, I have been guilty of making my plans and asking Jesus to bless them instead of asking Him for *His* plan.

Leaders who operate as I did tend to find themselves in a continuous state of frustration derived from not understanding why their great plans didn't produce the projected outcome. However, it must be understood that truly anointed ideas aren't the ones we come up with and then pray for Him to bless. Consistent life-changing ministry happens only when He speaks His heart to us in an atmosphere of intimacy.

This is why having an intimate relationship with Him is the key to overcoming the feeling that you should be there by now. How? Spiritual intimacy helps us see that *there* is actually *wherever He is*. This revelation will keep you from feeling as if you have to serve, or work, to get His attention and approval.

As I began to understand how I had overlooked my blind spot, I realized that my motivation to perform was based on the distance I felt between myself and Jesus. I had a continual need to get His attention by presenting my good works to Him.

In some ways, I acted like our cat, Charlie. Charlie is an outdoor cat that we allow into the house on occasion to be brushed and petted. From time to time, I'll step into our garage and discover a freshly killed rodent that Charlie has left as a prize for Gina and me. I don't know why cats do this. However, I understand it is normal cat behavior. I guess you could say cats are leaving us an offering.

I can now see that I allowed myself to become a lot like Charlie. I often left an offering of performance for Jesus in order to gain His approval. Deep down inside I believed I would get the big break I was hoping for if I could somehow offer some outstanding results. I thought I could unlock my potential by discovering that great idea that would finally validate my ministry. Or, like Charlie, maybe I could impress Him with my generous offering even though He never asked for it.

Can you see the destructive nature of performance? When ministry is based on your performance, it becomes more about what you can do instead of depending on Jesus to provide the plan and power necessary for sustained success. Operating this way leads to failure in some area. It's only through complete dependency on Him that we can experience a lasting and fruitful ministry.

IT'S ONLY THROUGH COMPLETE DEPENDENCY ON HIM THAT WE CAN EXPERIENCE A LASTING AND FRUITFUL MINISTRY.

I have heard this statement many times throughout the years: "We have to start well, run well, and finish well." The emphasis is on the importance of living a life of character and integrity throughout our journey. However, if we aren't careful, we can inadvertently put the focus on ourselves. The focus should not be on *our* ability to start, run, and finish. It should always be on daily making the choice of getting to know Jesus better. Just like Mary, I've discovered that true purpose and power are found by choosing that one essential of spending time with Him.

Have you ever wondered why many successful leaders fail morally? Even leaders with long ministry pedigrees and international influence have been removed from their positions of influence. How could they build something huge only to lose it many years later? The answer is really quite simple. They got so used to relying on their own abilities that they became disconnected from the true source of anointing—intimacy with

Him. Once this happens, it's only a matter of time before things begin to unravel. It is nearly impossible to have sustained effective ministry impact apart from His presence.

Friend, stop right now and take inventory of your own heart. Are you out of balance when it comes to serving versus sitting? Both are needed to be effective in ministry, but recall how we noted earlier that the *one* thing we need is to enjoy His presence. How encouraging to know that this opportunity won't be taken from you because it's essential.

Maybe the most important question is, What is most essential in your ministry? When I finally answered this question with transparent honesty, it brought tremendous breakthrough in my life. I sincerely pray the same thing for you.

HEALING ON THE FLY

Our oldest daughter, Tiffany, fell and scraped her elbow when she was a toddler. It was quite a traumatic experience for her at the time. However, Gina was able to bring miraculous healing to her boo-boo by putting a Band-Aid on it. Like most toddlers, Tiffany spent the next few days looking at her injury. She also made sure everyone she encountered knew about it too. Once the Band-Aid was removed, she continued to observe her boo-boo daily as if to monitor its healing process. One day, while walking and looking at her boo-boo, Tiffany walked right into our sliding glass door. Ouch. She had become so fixated on her injury that she slammed into an invisible wall right in front of her.

Tiffany's toddler experience describes thousands of pastors and other leaders in the church today. Can you relate? You may be carrying around some devastating wounds that still need healing. However, because of your daily responsibilities, the time to heal isn't available. So you continue leading as a wounded warrior. Eventually the outcome is the same as a toddler focusing on a boo-boo—you slam into a glass wall.

The results of focusing on our wounds are always the same. Inward focus stops momentum dead in its tracks. The larger ramification is this: an inward-focused leader always produces an inward-focused organization. Outreach and church growth cannot happen in such an environment.

This issue has given rise to a generation of pastors who have become doers instead of equippers. It's simply easier to carry out tasks while injured than risk being exposed while attempting to train others. A pastor's inward focus results in unhealthy codependency between the pastor and the congregation. The harder you work, the more you feel affirmed and significant, which temporarily eases your pain.

THERE IS NO SUCH THING AS HEALING ON THE FLY. THE

FIRST STEP TOWARD HEALING IS TO BECOME AWARE OF

THE REAL ISSUES. THEN WE CAN TAKE ACTION TOWARD

FREEDOM, GROWTH, AND FULFILLMENT.

Unfortunately, relating to your congregation in this fashion creates a dysfunctional church with an insider focus. The people in these churches are more concerned with having their needs met than with having an impact on their communities. Eventually insider-focused churches encounter certain death as they slam into the invisible wall of obscurity. In other words, although they are still in the community physically, their ability to influence the community dissolves. Once-thriving ministries fade into oblivion because they lose the ability to relate to those around them.

Pastoring is difficult. Our actions while caring for eternal souls have lasting consequences. Although we face many challenges, the hardest issue I dealt with while pastoring was having to grow and mature personally while still leading my congregation. Nothing made me feel more hypocritical than preaching or counseling on an issue I was personally struggling with. The machine of ministry never stopped making demands of me. It seemed as if I never had any time to withdraw and focus on my own health, let alone enter God's refreshing presence.

Many pastors struggle in this way. While we preach sermons about the benefits of Sabbath, we continue working seven days a week. We seldom practice what we preach. Sometimes this is because we refuse to slow down to rest and reflect. We can't take a time-out because we will spend that quiet time reviewing the results of our ministry. However, it's not just the workaholic pastor at fault here. Many of our congregations contribute to this problem as well. Their unrealistic expectations keep us spinning in this never-ending cycle.

Has your congregation ever required that you (or your staff) take time off to work on your marriage? Have they ever paid to send you and your spouse off for a week of restoration and replenishment? While some churches may be intentional about doing so, these practices rarely show up on the average church's radar. Our congregations can be quick to pounce on us if we have marriage problems or other issues, yet very seldom does a congregation invest in preventative measures to preserve and encourage the personal, physical, marital, and professional growth of their shepherds.

The cycle of unrealistic expectations soon causes us to find other ways to stimulate growth and present the appearance of a healthy congregation to the community. As is often the case, everything continues moving along in the same direction as long as it looks good.

It is easy to create the appearance of health in today's church culture because our society has become accustomed to churches that don't have a major impact on their communities. It seems that the main goal of a lot of churches is to blend in with the local culture. I call them chameleon churches. They simply take on the characteristics of their surroundings.

This path usually leads pastors to embrace a destructive practice. Out of sheer desperation, we allow our ministries to be driven by hype. Hype can manifest itself in many ways. It's not always about being louder, flashier, or more cutting edge. Sometimes hype involves attempting to be deeper, smarter, or more refined than others. Regardless of how it's implemented, it has the same results.

A friend of mine used to say, "You can't sustain hype." There has never been a truer statement. The hype-driven ministry is faced with a perpetual challenge—you have to come up with something next week to "out-hype" what you did this week. The hype cycle never ends. It doesn't take long to discover that your ministry becomes shallow when you're hype driven. Additionally, you lose credibility with everyone. The elders become wary, the staff gets worn out, the volunteers run for the hills, and the congregation eventually looks for a more authentic worship experience elsewhere.

It becomes apparent to everyone that it's time for a change in leadership when the hype-driven ministry comes to a halt. The promises you made haven't panned out. The growth you anticipated hasn't materialized. When this happens, everyone you have been leading develops a lasting distrust of you. Broken trust leads to broken relationships. If left undealt with, this blind spot will deal a blow to your leadership that is hard to overcome.

Continuing to overlook this blind spot only worsens our injured condition. As is true with any physical ailment, healing requires us to stop and deal with our injury. There is no such thing as healing on the fly. The first step toward healing is to become aware of the real issues. Then we can take action toward freedom, growth, and fulfillment.

DIGGING DEEPER

1. Are you living with an unhealed wound? In what ways does that affect your ministry?

2. Has the lack of church growth caused you to become inward focused? What is one thing you could do immediately to shift your focus outward?

3. What blind spot might you have overlooked because you have become accustomed to leading a ministry that isn't making an impact on your community?

4. What is one action you can take this week to begin healing and move toward dependency on God rather than your own efforts?

5. Name the ways you have defaulted to become a hype-driven ministry. What are some changes you need to make in order to lead more effectively?

3

UNFULFILLED

The world is changed by your example, not by your opinion.

—Paulo Coelho

Do you ever reflect on why you are in the ministry? I think about it a lot. It's humbling to understand that I am a representative of Jesus who is charged with connecting our culture to the good news. It's a little sobering too. I take my calling as seriously as you take yours.

Looking back over the past three decades, I'm thankful for the experiences I have had. Opportunities such as leading a traveling music group, doing promotions at a large radio station, church planting on a major college campus, being a consultant for the Unstuck Group, and serving in about every staff position imaginable in the local church shaped me into who I am today.

However, none of those activities compare to serving as a lead pastor of a small church. Sure, there were good times and bad. Yes, there were a lot of days when I asked myself why I was doing this. Yet no matter the obstacles I faced, I had unquenchable joy and passion to change the world for Jesus. I knew in my heart that my life was going to have a lasting impact and make a big difference. After all, doesn't every leader feel this way?

I have always been enamored with big endeavors. It really doesn't matter what arena it's in. It just has to have a large-scale impact. In my mind, bigger was always better, so it was only natural to believe that Jesus had big plans for my life. All I needed to do was say yes and the doors were going to swing open. Right? As naive as it sounds now, this is close to how I viewed the future. After all, there were a lot of successful ministries all around the nation. Surely Jesus was planning for mine to become one of them.

A STARTLING DISCOVERY

During our season of traveling with music groups, I discovered an alarming trend in many churches. Our schedule usually allowed a few minutes to pray with the pastor or a staff member from the host church before the concert. During these prayer times, I noticed a common theme would surface. Most of the leaders were really discouraged.

This didn't just happen occasionally. It actually was the norm. Church after church. Concert after concert. One leader to the next. The discouragement these leaders were dealing with astounded me. I wondered how so many great men and women of God could be that beaten down and disillusioned with ministry. Where did their passion go? In the years ahead, the source of this discouragement became clear to me. Something had ambushed them on the inside.

Does this sound familiar to you? In an atmosphere of safety and transparency, if you could be completely honest, would you confess you are really disheartened? Do you feel so unfulfilled that your passion has begun to fade? Has your desire to make a difference given way to despair? Or, even worse, has the belief that you can have an impact on your community left you completely?

In case you're not sure, let me give you some common examples of the personal costs that drain our emotional accounts. In an article titled "Pastor Stress Statistics," Bill Gaultiere provided the following information:

RESEARCH ON PASTORS' WELL-BEING

Many research studies have been done on pastors' stress, spiritual life, marriage, and family. In this article I summarize key results from more than ten studies and cite the source for each statistic. Also I suggest that the negative effects of ministry on the well-being of pastors and their families is probably due to a combination of stress overload and inadequate personal soul care.

STATISTICS ON PASTORS' MINISTRY STRESS

Why aren't these pastors overflowing with the love, joy and peace of the Lord in their lives, families and ministries? What is the cause of their emotional problems and moral failures? A major factor is overwhelming ministry stress:

- 75% of pastors report being "extremely stressed" or "highly stressed"
- 90% work between 55 to 75 hours per week
- 90% feel fatigued and worn out every week
- 70% say they're grossly underpaid
- 40% report a serious conflict with a parishioner at least once a month
- 78% were forced to resign from their church (63% at least twice), most commonly because of church conflict
- 80% will not be in ministry ten years later and only a fraction make it a lifelong career. On

average, seminary trained pastors last only five
years in church ministry

100% of 1,050 Reformed and Evangelical pastors
had a colleague who had left the ministry
because of burnout, church conflict, or moral
failure

91% have experienced some form of burnout in
ministry and 18% say they are "fried to a crisp
right now"

STATISTICS ON PASTORS' EMOTIONAL HEALTH, FAMILY, AND MORALITY

It's particularly disturbing to see how much pastors are struggling with emotional pain, family problems, loving well, and
moral failures:

70% of pastors say they have a lower self-esteem now
than when they entered ministry

70% constantly fight depression

50% feel so discouraged that they would leave
their ministry if they could, but can't find
another job

80% believe their pastoral ministry has negatively
affected their families and 33% said it was an
outright hazard

80% of ministry spouses feel left out and
unappreciated in their church

77% feel they do not have a good marriage

41% display anger problems in marriage (reported
by the spouse)

38% are divorced or divorcing

50% admit to using pornography and 37% report
   inappropriate sexual behavior with someone in
   the church

65% feel their family is in a glass house

STATISTICS ON PASTORS' LACK OF SOUL CARE AND TRAINING

But ministry stress alone does not explain why pastors burnout emotionally or blow out morally. Other statistics suggest that many pastors struggle with "professionalizing" their spiritual lives and failing to care for their own souls under God:

53% of pastors do not feel that seminary or Bible
   college prepared them adequately

70% do not have someone they consider a close
   friend

50% do not meet regularly with an accountability
   person or group

72% only study the Bible when preparing for
   sermons or lessons

21% spend less than 15 minutes a day in prayer—
   the average is 39 minutes per day

16% are "very satisfied" with their prayer life, 47%
   are "somewhat satisfied," and 37% are either
   "somewhat dissatisfied" or "very dissatisfied"
   (spending more time in quiet prayer or
   listening to God versus making requests was
   correlated with higher satisfaction)

44% of pastors do not take a regular day off

31% do not exercise at all, while 37% exercise at
   least three or four days a week as recommended

> 90% say they have not received adequate training
> to meet the demands of ministry
> 85% have never taken a Sabbatical[6]

Serving in ministry can slowly and methodically deplete your passion. As you reflect on ways you have been blindsided by ministry, consider what price you have had to pay. Do you feel like a shell of the person you were when you started? Some common habits and thought patterns keep our ministries from turning out as we hoped. Here are a few:

Competition: We blame the larger ministries in town for stealing our people.

Contemplation: We consistently talk more of what God did instead of what God is doing.

Comparison: We define and measure our success against other ministries.

Constraints: We focus on our needs instead of the Source of our provision.

Complacency: We have become resigned to having little kingdom impact.

If these practices have become part of your daily thoughts and conversations, then you probably have also thought you would be there by now. However, the real issue you need to confront may be that you have embraced the wrong definition of success. It is easy to develop a wrong definition of success when you've been blindsided by self-doubt. Unchecked, self-doubt can take up residence inside you and eat away at you like a slow-growing cancer.

Self-doubt isn't reserved just for leaders of small churches. Many successful leaders of larger ministries grapple with the question of "What now?" They have taken their organizations to new heights. However, each new pinnacle reached also reveals the next one to pursue. It often feels as if the peace that should come with reaching new heights is unattainable. To make matters worse, these leaders also come to understand that they now have to learn a new set of leadership principles to get to the next level. This entire process can be exhausting and unfulfilling.

If you've been in ministry for very long, you know in your heart that the actions that got you where you are now will not get you to the next destination. And if you don't change your thinking and your habits, then in all likelihood, you will perpetuate an unhealthy ministry that will not grow. The ripple effect of an ongoing unhealthy ministry can last for several generations. Now is the time for us to come together and get the help we need. Your church, not to mention the world around you, needs you now more than ever.

LEADING ON EMPTY

Exhaustion is the common denominator in every major mistake I have made in my adult life. Without exception, I was physically, mentally, and spiritually exhausted at each of these times. Exhaustion will always lead us to give up the fight. We were not created to press on full steam ahead every day of our lives. Craig D. Lounsbrough said, "We tediously create calendars filled with empty duties, and then we foolishly let those calendars empty us."[7] I hate admitting that I have been guilty of doing this.

You've heard the old parental cliché "Do what I say and not what I do." If you're like me, you go ahead and do what they do. While most pastors do a good job of living what they preach, I have identified one area in which most pastors tend to ignore the instruction of Scripture. Pastors find it easier to teach about observing the Sabbath than to actually practice taking a day off to rest.

We do this for many reasons. Some of us believe it's part of our call as pastors to sacrifice our health for the people in our congregations. Others need to be seen as martyrs in order to fulfill a need for acceptance. Still other pastors are so driven that they justify ignoring a clear directive from God about observing a Sabbath. Whatever the motivator, nothing will cause us to lose perspective faster than exhaustion. A pastor continuing to operate despite having lost perspective will eventually bring an entire ministry to an abrupt halt.

One summer several years ago, Gina and I spent a vacation with some friends at their lake house. As the week came to an end, we decided to head home in time to attend church on Sunday morning. After loading the car, I decided it would be fun to squeeze in a casual Sunday morning ride on the water before loading the boat onto the trailer. So we jumped into the boat on this picture-perfect morning and took off. The lake was especially smooth at this early hour since no other boats were on the water yet.

The ride was so peaceful and relaxing. Although I was keeping tabs on the time, I neglected to focus on how far we had traveled. But once I recognized the interstate bridge as we came around a bend, I realized we had traveled over two miles. Just as we turned around to head back to the lake house, the boat began to sputter with the unmistakable sound that accompanies an empty fuel tank. I had uncharacteristically forgotten to check the fuel level in my haste to squeeze in one more ride. We were now dead in the water over two miles from our destination. And there was not a soul in sight. I have never felt so embarrassed. Or hopeless.

Our options of what to do next were limited.

Option one: We could jump into the lake and swim to shore with the boat in tow. However, we were sitting in the widest part of the lake. Also, we'd still be two miles from the lake house even if we made it to land.

Option two: We could start paddling. I should mention that we had only one short paddle, which required extensive stretching over the side of the boat to gain traction. And, of course, the morning sun was now beating down on us.

We chose option two … and it was brutal. By now a slight breeze had kicked up, and the current was fighting against us. We were working as hard as we could without making any progress. I've never experienced a more stressful situation. The stress wasn't just because of our current problem. It was much more than that to me. How could I have been so careless? My actions didn't affect just me. My poor wife had to help paddle a boat for two miles because of her husband's bad decision.

SOME OF US ACTUALLY BELIEVE THAT JESUS HAS CALLED US TO LIVES OF *INDEPENDENCE*. YET, IN REALITY, OUR FOCUS SHOULD BE HEALTHY *INTERDEPENDENCE*.

Does this situation sound familiar? Many pastors and other leaders all across America find themselves in a similar place. What began as a hopeful journey together has completely stalled. The organization is now dead in the water. In some instances, it was our leadership decisions, either through action or inaction, that contributed to the problem. The resulting pressure building around us soon became the stress within us. Proverbs 13:12 describes how I felt most days: "Unrelenting disappointment leaves you heartsick, but a sudden good break can turn life around."

Does leading your church feel as if you're swimming to shore with a boat in tow? Or like paddling against the current for miles without making any progress? Whatever your situation, you simply can't continue leading in this fashion. The internal weight you are carrying, coupled with the external pressures, ultimately proves to be too much to bear. The pressure cooker you're living in soon causes you to question your calling. The anticipated fulfillment of ministry success is replaced by the unfulfillment that accompanies being stalled. Over time I began to recognize the link between feeling unfulfilled and being distracted.

To this day I wonder why I didn't check the fuel tank on the boat. It's not normal for me to make such an avoidable mistake. I do remember thinking it would be best if we just loaded up the boat and headed home. But I allowed my desire to squeeze one more thing into our schedule to distract me. This distraction led to a disastrous situation. I felt like a failure.

I believe there is nothing more difficult for a leader to deal with than failure. Leaders hate to fail. For pastors, the pressure is even greater because we know that everything we do is out in the open for all to see. It has been said that the good things a pastor does look better than they really are. And the bad things a pastor does look worse than they really are. Unfortunately, it goes with the territory of being out in front of people consistently.

The problem of failure is compounded by the fact that most pastors have a deep-seated drive that can often distort the balance required to be a healthy leader. There is no greater calling on earth than shepherding people. It is both a great privilege and a heavy responsibility. The results of our actions carry the weight of eternal consequences. Truthfully, the pressure of pastoring never subsides.

THE MOTIVE OF THE INTERDEPENDENT LEADER IS TO HELP PEOPLE FIND FULFILLMENT BY LIVING OUT THEIR PURPOSE.

This reality is why it is so important for you as a pastor to discover and consistently experience the benefits of kingdom principles such as Sabbath rest, healthy margin, and dependency. The underlying theme in each of these concepts is that we can't do it alone. Most pastors agree intellectually that we can't do it alone, but we tend to cave in to the expectations of those around us as well as our own. Before we know it, we're attempting to handle everything ourselves—alone. Some of us actually believe that Jesus has called us to lives of *independence*. Yet, in reality, our focus should be healthy *interdependence*.

As equippers, interdependence is at the core of our calling and purpose. An interdependent leader knows that equipping can't be done in a vacuum. It requires interaction, a hands-on approach, if you will. This leader takes the time to get to know people and find out how God uniquely created them. This requires follow-through and patience. The motive of the interdependent leader is to help people find fulfillment by living out their purpose.

Independent leaders, however, often seem to create avenues for service in order to find people to carry out *their* vision. They recruit people to fill gaps instead of training people to use their gifts. This is where a lot of leadership training is either misunderstood or misappropriated. While it is true that great leaders get things done through others, the goal of great leadership isn't isolation. The goal is building a healthy team that we lead while walking alongside them.

Equipping has never been about training people and then turning them loose, never to be seen again. Equipping is more about helping people use their gifts to grow God's kingdom. As their pastor, you get a front-row seat to watch them find their place. In reality, equipping is a lot like coaching. When it's done well, everyone is a winner.

When our focus is healthy interdependence, Satan cannot derail us with the temptation of doing ministry alone. However, he can stall us out if he entices us in areas where we already struggle. Thankfully, though, God has put several warning signs in place to keep us from becoming stalled.

By studying 1 Kings 17–19, we can see the warning signs that preceded Elijah stalling out. You can probably relate to them.

WARNING SIGN 1: DOING MINISTRY ALONE

Elijah did ministry alone in his early years. He did have a servant, but he didn't have a team of co-laborers. Nothing dampens your passion and optimism more than feeling as if you are on your own when it comes to leading a church. Leading volunteers is one of the hardest jobs anyone will ever face. But it's far better than going it alone.

WARNING SIGN 2: LACK OF CONGREGATIONAL COMMITMENT

The weight Elijah carried from seeing how far off track God's people had become is heartbreaking. Spiritual leaders are not perfect, nor do we claim to be. However, we are sometimes dumbfounded by the actions of people in our congregations and their lack of conviction at times. Nothing in ministry contributed to the stress I experienced more than this. Seeing the poor decisions that family, friends, church members, and even fellow leaders made in direct opposition to God's Word often left me speechless. And it also caused me to examine my own leadership.

You might wonder why you would examine your leadership. It's because when pastors are leading on empty, they tend to blame themselves for the decisions of others. It's common to think, *That person probably would not have made such a bad decision if I were a better leader.*

WARNING SIGN 3: FRUSTRATION FROM NEEDING TO GO BACK AND REBUILD

Elijah immediately had to go back to rebuild instead of moving forward to build something new. He knew he had to take the people back to the foundational principles of the faith before he could take them forward. This is why the Bible says in 1 Kings 18:30, "Elijah told the people, 'Enough of that—it's my turn. Gather around.' And they gathered. He then put the altar back together for by now it was in ruins."

Frustration and discouragement can develop when you're leading difficult people. You realize you're going to need to spend a great deal of time and energy on the fundamentals. It's frustrating because you want to show the people where you plan to take them and then head out. But every good leader knows it's a waste of time to blaze a new trail without addressing the unresolved issues that led to being stalled in the first place.

EVERY GOOD LEADER KNOWS IT'S A WASTE OF TIME TO BLAZE A NEW TRAIL WITHOUT ADDRESSING THE UNRESOLVED ISSUES THAT LED TO BEING STALLED IN THE FIRST PLACE.

I had a pastor friend many years ago who experienced this firsthand. He had accepted the job of leading a new church with a great deal of expectancy and hope of making a huge impact. However, he soon realized he had inherited a staff and congregation who were extremely dysfunctional and injured. Every attempt he made to implement anything new was met with antagonism, distrust, and resistance.

As he sincerely sought the Lord for a solution, he sensed Him telling him in prayer one morning, "You are going to have to go back before you can go forward." My friend knew that moving forward without addressing the baggage of the past would simply bring the same baggage into the future.

WARNING SIGN 4: REFUSING TO REPLENISH

Being used by God to bring about a national revival drained Elijah. It's fascinating to me that he became so intimidated by Jezebel's threat that he ran for his life (19:2–3). Remember, he had just called fire down from heaven to consume the sacrifice and then killed all her false prophets. At this point, why would her threats concern him? The answer is simple. He was exhausted.

It is impossible to remain effective in ministry while simultaneously running on fumes. The major mistakes I have made as an adult always happened when I was exhausted. In the majority of my missteps, a direct correlation always existed between a lack of clear thinking and exhaustion.

Any pastor who continues to ignore these warning signs will end up stalled in ministry. Even the prophet Elijah dealt with some of these issues. I find it helpful to know that a man whom God used in such incredible ways also had some problems. You may have discovered this truth: your ministry can be the thing that destroys your ministry.

WAYS TO AVOID THE WARNING SIGNS

BUILD A HEALTHY TEAM

Make this your first priority. If you're like most pastors, attendance numbers really affect you. I understand. However, I encourage you to shift your focus toward measuring health instead of counting people. The truth is, if your church is unhealthy, you will only be adding to the problem by adding people. But if you can achieve health through building a competent team around you, then you will also create a structure that can handle steady growth. The sharper the team you build, the greater your potential for sustained growth. You will also find greater fulfillment in raising up others to do the work instead of doing it all by yourself.

In case team building is something you need help with, allow me to share the basics from a resource I created for 95Nework titled "Eight Key Principles for Equipping Saints and Improving Follow-Through."

1. Make your mission plain. Simply put, your mission explains *why* you exist as a ministry. There is no better way to communicate it to your volunteers than to put it in writing. You can also make a practice of writing down more specific objectives. This will bring clarity and remove any possible misunderstanding. Instructions not written down seldom get followed.

2. When possible, match roles with giftedness. This practice is not always possible in a small church due to the limited volunteer pool. However, as you grow, it is important to remember that people tend to follow through and serve faithfully when the mission connects with their passion and gifts. Try connecting people with their passion when possible.

3. Equip leaders with tools for success. Nothing brings greater frustration to volunteers than to be asked to do something without being given the resources to accomplish the task. They feel set up for failure from the start. It is better not to start an initiative than to launch something without the tools for success.

4. Resist the urge to manipulate and intimidate. It still amazes me to see how many leaders use manipulation and intimidation to run organizations. Not only does this leadership style wear out the volunteers, it also wears out the leader. Guilt and hype are only temporary ways to motivate people.

5. Release responsibilities incrementally. Jesus taught the principle that faithfulness over a little leads to more responsibility (Luke 16:10). As desperate as you are for volunteers, don't allow yourself to release too much too fast to new volunteers. Overwhelmed volunteers will eventually quit.

6. Identify leaders of teams and empower them. Remember when Moses's father-in-law advised him to share his load (Ex. 18:14–23)? His advice was predicated on empowering leaders based on their ability to handle leadership at certain levels. Paul told Timothy to release leadership to followers who were both faithful and able (2 Tim. 2:2). Once you have identified and recruited your leaders, it is imperative that you let them lead. Micromanagement will only lead to turnover.

7. Inspect what you expect. One of the difficulties of leading a volunteer organization is that you can never *assume* that folks will follow through. However, this reality does not mean you need to be cynical or down on your people. It just means you have to constantly stay in tune with your leaders to make sure things are running smoothly. Good communication is not always about passing or failing. Sometimes it's simply about tweaking and offering direction in order to achieve your goals.

8. Provide positive reinforcement. Great leaders are awesome encouragers. We should always make it our goal as leaders to be the biggest cheerleaders and supporters for both volunteers and staff members. I once had a pastor I worked for who would personally hand out our paychecks every two weeks. He always said, "Thank you for being a part of our team." That encouragement meant so much to me. I would have done anything to help him fulfill our church's vision!

Implementing these eight equipping principles will foster an atmosphere of consistent community and follow-through. Just remember that the best growth happens incrementally.

Special note: It's so important for you as a small church leader to understand that you simply can't offer everything larger ministries offer. The lack of resources and people makes it impossible. So the best thing to do is scale back to doing a few things really well. Your impact will be much greater if you do a few things well than if you attempt to do a lot of things poorly.

TRUST GOD WITH THE RESULTS

This may be the hardest lesson I had to learn. I always took it personally when those under my care would mess up their lives. My guilt came from thinking that if I had only preached better or prayed more or led differently, they would not have walked away from God, their marriages, or their families. Pastor, you cannot allow the poor decisions of the people you lead to devastate you. Your calling is to faithfully deliver the message and leave the results up to God.

TAKE TIME FOR HONEST ASSESSMENTS

Many pastors arrive at a new church with an inaccurate perception of the congregation. It's not necessarily the pastor's fault. We are often misled about the true condition of the church during the interview process. We accept the position, thinking our new congregation is ready to pull together to reach the surrounding communities. However, what we soon discover are power struggles, wrong motives, and a great deal of spiritual immaturity that must be confronted before any new action plan can be implemented. The "honeymoon" season quickly becomes the "punched in the gut" season.

It is imperative to have an honest evaluation of the current situation no matter how ugly it may be. I suggest bringing in an outside strategic planning process, similar to 95Network's VisionDay, which can provide an unbiased set of fresh eyes to lead the team through the steps. Bad facts are better in the long run than good intentions.

DO NOT BECOME ANOTHER STATISTIC

I have witnessed several influential leaders experience moral failure. As news of their bad choices became public, I was shaken to the core. I deeply respected their ministry success. *How can I possibly be faithful when someone I held in such high esteem could fall?* That question haunted me day and night. I often experienced mental fatigue from hoping I would not make the same mistakes they did.

Remaining faithful throughout your ministry won't happen by chance. You must develop daily, weekly, monthly, and annual plans to set aside time for replenishment, recovery, and refocusing. Setting aside this time does not happen automatically! You must literally write down these plans in your calendar. Make yourself accountable to a trusted elder in the church to check up on how you are doing in honoring your need for rest.

In case you're wondering how things turned out for Gina and me on the lake, we were fine. After paddling for an hour or so, we noticed a single boat on the water, headed in our direction. The driver pulled up beside us and offered help. Although he didn't have any spare fuel, he instead suggested something we found unbelievable: he would tow us wherever we needed. He didn't even flinch when I told him how far it was to our lake house. We were so relieved and humbled. He tied a ski rope to our boat and began the slow journey of pulling us back to where we started.

Have you ever experienced that amount of underserved grace? If so, you can probably relate to what I was feeling. Here was a complete stranger taking time out of his day to help us. I was thankful while simultaneously battling shame because my poor decision got us stranded in the first place. I was also flooded with the peace and presence of the Spirit of God as He reminded me how dependent on Him I really am. It was a deeply moving experience.

First Kings 19:19–21 shows us how God sent help to Elijah when he reached the end of his rope. He appointed Elisha to take over his ministry. The Bible later reveals that Elisha inherited a double portion of Elijah's anointing (2 Kings 2:9–12). After regaining a proper prospective, Elijah left a next-generation leader equipped to faithfully carry on and expand what he had started.

I will always acknowledge my need for the grace of God in order to accomplish what He has called me to do. Anything less than grace would only be a futile attempt to do things in my own strength. Relying on my abilities to accomplish what He has called me to do will leave me stalled in the water.

FROM HIM INSTEAD OF FOR HIM

When I began to understand how unhealthy I was, I finally opened up to receiving help. Before that, I never seriously considered reaching out to anyone, because it seemed to signal weakness. I have met a lot of pastors who tend to avoid anything that would expose a crack in their armor—even the slightest hint of one. I think we maintain that image for a couple of reasons.

First, we are so driven to perform that we never slow down long enough to realize that our behavior has become unhealthy.

Second, we intentionally try to stay busy doing the Lord's work in order to keep anyone from finding out we're hurting.

Whatever the reason, for many years I resisted giving any sign that I needed help. Fortunately, Jesus connected me with someone who pointed me down the road to healing.

Bob Hamp is a counselor from the Dallas area. I was introduced to his teaching when he was leading the Freedom Ministry at Gateway Church in Southlake, Texas. A fellow pastor had recommended a short video by Bob titled "The Problem Jesus Came to Solve."[8] (We will dive deeper into the main emphasis of this video in the third section of this book.) Bob gave one simple illustration that had a great impact on me, and I want to share it with you.

Bob suggested that God's interaction with Adam at creation might have gone like this: God said to Adam, "I'll run the heavens; you run the earth. Everything will work perfectly as long as you stay connected to Me." God intended to get His kingdom plans operating in the earth by flowing *through* us.

This illustration really got my attention. It confronted my belief that I needed to do things *for* God. We even see Jesus saying in the Lord's Prayer, "Your kingdom come, your will be done, on earth as it is in heaven" (Matt. 6:10 NIV).

Bob went on to say that I can't actually do things *for* God because there is nothing God needs. And if God did need anything, it would be quite presumptuous for me to think I could provide it. He said that God intended for me to do things *from* Him. Let that sink in for a moment …

God's original design was for me to do things *from* Him, not *for* Him.

To do things *from* Him is to let the Holy Spirit speak to me and then to obey His direction. Each of us was created with a specific purpose and the gifts necessary to fulfill this purpose. As we grow in intimacy with Jesus, we develop the ability to hear His voice more clearly. Therefore, we are able to react to His direction with reflex obedience. Doing ministry *from* Him gives freshness to our daily walk with the Lord. It flows from choosing the one essential thing—enjoying His presence.

The pressure to perform went out the window as I embraced that God's design for me was to do things *from* Him, not *for* Him. It has never been, nor will it ever be, my responsibility to change someone's life. Only He can do that. Do you see how ministry-changing this concept can be?

Imagine with me for a minute that we are in your favorite coffee shop discussing this topic of doing ministry from God instead of for Him. Looking around the coffee shop, we see the barista intensely filling orders for the other patrons in the room. He has all the latest equipment, which allows him to satisfy his loyal customers' requests time and time again. It is important to make sure the equipment is state of the art in order to keep up with the competition. That is just the price of having a successful coffee business.

However, something else can make or break the functionality of even the most expensive equipment: the coffee machine must be plugged in to an electrical outlet. Whether in the coffee shop or in my kitchen, things designed to be plugged in will not work without a power source.

Even if you and I have the knowledge, training, talents, spiritual gifts, experience, and right attitude to accomplish amazing things for Jesus, we could fail to realize our potential because we don't connect to the source of true ministry power.

I don't want to see this happen to you in your ministry. I get that your discouragement is real. Honestly, my concern for you isn't as much for *how* you got here as it is for *where* you go from here. Maybe you've been trying to do things *for* God up until now. And the costs have been high for you and your family. But now you've realized it's time to plug into the power source in order to live life *from* Him.

Take a moment right now and think about it ... What if you're missing out on a life of effective ministry because you're playing it safe by holding on to what you have always done? Maybe the problem is not so much about what is happening *around* you. What if the problem is really more about what is happening *in* you? If that's true, then it's wonderful news because now you can do something about it.

EFFECTIVE MINISTRY IS MORE ABOUT WHAT JESUS CAN DO

THROUGH US THAN WHAT WE CAN DO *FOR* HIM.

Let this concept sink in. The megaministry down the street is not your problem. A lack of resources is not your problem. No other outside issue is the real problem. The real problem is that we have stopped believing that Jesus can do anything *through* us. Pastor, now would be a good time to remember that He is "able to do exceedingly abundantly above all that we ask or think, *according to the power that works in us*" (Eph. 3:20 NKJV, emphasis added).

Effective ministry is more about what Jesus can do *through* us than what we can do *for* Him. Our churches are in desperate need of leaders who no longer minister *for* Jesus but instead minister *from* Jesus.

In the coming chapters, we are going to look at several ways to help you gain clarity on how to choose His power daily. Nothing is more fulfilling than ministering with God's power driving the results.

DIGGING DEEPER

1. Are you ready to have a significant change in your ministry? What change would you most like to see in your church?

2. Do you need to plug into the source of God's power by following Mary's example? What made you realize this need?

3. How would it impact your ministry if you chose the one essential element that will not be taken from you?

4. Describe several ways in which you can begin doing ministry *from* God instead of *for* Him.

5. Define what it means for you to allow His power to work in you. What are some steps you can take each day to become a greater conduit of His power?

SECTION 2

WHAT WILL I FIND THERE?

THE LOOK OF THE PRESENT

My friend Dan and I were trying to recover a deer one Saturday evening. As we crisscrossed a two-thousand-acre forest of pines, dusk quickly became pitch-black night. Soon, to put it in southern terms, I was good and lost. I had allowed myself to become so obsessed with finding my trophy that I failed to pay attention to where I was. Once I noticed that Dan's flashlight was nowhere in sight, I made the startling discovery that rows of pines all look the same in the dark. I was turned around and starting to panic a little.

In that unsettling moment, I remembered some wise instruction I had received as a child: "If you ever get lost in the woods, just stay put and let your rescuers find you." The wisdom here is that it's much easier for someone who knows the way to locate you if you don't wander deeper into the woods. This is such good advice.

Have you ever felt so lost? I've noticed that whenever I feel lost, insecure, or exposed, I tend to think back to childhood. I wonder if this is a defense mechanism that only I default to or if other people experience it as well. I usually see the seven-year-old version of myself trying to navigate my way through the situation. I guess it's possible that I'm looking for my father's help.

I can't recall a time from childhood when my dad rescued me. I hesitate to write this because I don't want to misrepresent my dad at all. He and I were close, and I don't intend to be critical of him. I simply can't remember any scenarios in which he rescued me—or failed to rescue me. My memory is blank.

This reality may reveal why I have often felt on my own in my relationship with my heavenly Father. In difficult situations, I tend to feel abandoned, left to figure things out for myself, because I have no expectation of rescue. So instead of patiently waiting for His help, my inclination has been to keep on moving—which has only made situations worse. The rescue I needed in that dark forest would have been much easier to experience if I had waited for help.

Acting on the wisdom I gleaned from childhood ultimately led to reconnecting with Dan that night in the woods. I have to admit I was really thankful for the darkness because I was able to hide my embarrassment in the shadows of the night. Any illumination would have revealed my *look of shame* for getting lost in the first place.

This section is designed to help you uncover where you are currently. We will approach some topics that have most likely caused the *look* you currently wear. This *look* reveals that you think you have failed and that failure defines you. The topics of traits, transition, and transformation require a fresh approach from an open heart, which will help you find your way out of the woods.

Whether you are aware of it or not, how you respond to each of them will have a profound impact on your ability to fulfill your calling. Could it be that you have been so focused on finding what's waiting *there* that you have failed to pay attention to how you got *here*?

As we proceed, I invite you to consider that you may have allowed some wrong concepts to shape your thinking. It's going to get personal. Like me, you may have adopted ideas and beliefs that are more traditional than biblical, which may be what brought you to this point in your ministry. I know how hard it is to admit that my thinking may be my problem. Yet unaddressed, these misconceptions perpetuate your inability to see an alternate path that could lead you out of the woods and into your God-given calling.

If wandering around in the massive forest of ministry has caused you to develop the *lost look*, then let's work together to help you clearly see the way out.

4

TRAITS

Indecisive leaders, who need to please everyone, end up pleasing no one.

—Dan Rockwell, "5 Ways to Become a Healthy People-Pleaser"

Over time each of us develops certain traits in our personalities that are derived from our upbringing and experiences. These attributes determine how we act in the various situations we face. They also reveal how we feel about ourselves as leaders.

In this chapter we'll look at three areas that influence why you and I do the things we do. Understanding them will help to correct any negative aspects of their impact on our lives today.

The task ahead is quite daunting. The fact that we are under a well-orchestrated attack from hell coupled with several hundred years of church tradition makes traveling the road ahead a scary proposition. It's not for the faint of heart, but you probably wouldn't be reading this book if you weren't ready for massive change. You realize that solid leadership is a must going forward.

It would be much easier for you to repeat the same excuses that many denominational leaders and pastors use in order to maintain the status quo. However, I beg you to go against the tide of compromise. You are not that far from arriving *there*. It is possible that everything you have experienced in thinking you would be there by now has been preparing you to join a movement. Jesus is recruiting pastors and other leaders who will allow Him to work through them to bring about the greatest move of God the world has ever seen.

Leading the church where it needs to go in the next few decades will exact a heavy price from you. You will be misunderstood, misrepresented, and maligned. Your integrity will be questioned, your abilities challenged, and your energy drained. There is certainly no guarantee of success. In fact, recent church history would suggest failure is imminent. So why even try?

When opposition knocks, I invite you to ask yourself, *What's at stake if I don't try?*

Jerry Bostick, flight dynamics officer for the Apollo 13 mission, was once asked, "Weren't there times when everybody, or at least a few people, just panicked?" He answered, "No, when bad things happened, we just calmly laid out all the options, and *failure was not one of them.* We never panicked, and we never gave up on finding a solution."[9] For the movie *Apollo 13* years later, screenwriters Al Reinert and Bill Broyles tweaked Bostick's words to "Failure is not an option" and gave them to Gene Kranz, flight director of Gemini and Apollo missions.

What impact could we have on our world if we believed failure was not an option? I am just as inspired by the second sentence: "We never panicked, and we never gave up on finding a solution." I can say with great confidence that our heavenly Flight Instructor has a solution to every problem we will confront. We just need to study the Manual, do what it says, and never give up on finding the solution.

Doing what we've always done must be replaced with fresh thinking. We must develop a strategy to work together cross-generationally in order to change our nation. Pastor, someone is going to have to step up and lead this change. I believe God is calling you.

APPROVAL AND ACCEPTANCE

It seems that many of us are in the ministry because we see it as a place to gain approval from others. When I was pastoring a small church, if I felt successful, it was easy to offer approval to others. On the other hand, when I failed to reach a goal, I often resented others who appeared to have accomplished more than I had.

My friend Dan Lian and I discussed this topic one morning over coffee. "I think it's fair to say that many of us from all walks of life suffer from some form of a father wound," Dan observed. "In reality, all of us probably have a father wound that we either have worked through or are working through. This wound tends to drive us to find approval so we can finally receive recognition for what we have accomplished."

Dan went on to say, "However, ministry was never meant to be a journey to find approval. It's actually meant to be spent showing others what it means to be approved. Ministry becomes an idol when its main objective in our hearts is to fulfill our need for approval."

Dan and I agreed that this insatiable desire for approval isn't limited to the small-church pastor. The driving force behind the success and then ultimate failure of many larger-ministry leaders may be the same desire for approval. When allowed to flourish in our hearts, the need for approval affects us in much the same way as a drug. Our highs and lows directly correlate to whether we are able to satisfy the desire for approval. It's possible to become an approval junkie.

Left unchecked, our need for approval can soon become an addiction. Denying that approval addiction has control of you will lead to a dark place that is increasingly difficult to come back from. It has nothing to do with whether you love God or not. It's all about whether the need for approval has taken control of your life. It eventually progresses into an idol when it's allowed to gain a stronghold in your heart.

MINISTRY WAS NEVER MEANT TO BE A JOURNEY TO FIND

APPROVAL. IT'S ACTUALLY MEANT TO BE SPENT SHOW-

ING OTHERS WHAT IT MEANS TO BE APPROVED.

Approval addiction can manifest itself in many ways. But no matter how it surfaces, it always reveals a level of insecurity. A need for affirmation and a resistance to accountability are often found at the core of approval addiction.

You might wonder what deficiency this behavior is exposing. And specifically, as pastors and other spiritual leaders, what void are we trying to fill with this addiction to approval? My answer may surprise you. Simply put, in so many cases, we have never been able to receive approval and acceptance from Father God.

I'm not referring to your theology, doctrine, or training. I'm sure you do a masterful job of teaching how human beings can be in right standing with God because of the sacrifice of Jesus. Therefore, this thought isn't intended to challenge your understanding of His Word. It's designed to challenge your understanding of His heart toward you.

What I'm referring to is learning how to live the abundant life that Jesus promised us (John 10:10). Many pastors have spent years teaching the principle of the abundant life. However, we also have succumbed to a belief that there must be more we should be doing as pastors. This can cause us to reason that He really had hoped to get more out of us during our short time here on earth. As I revealed earlier, I spent the majority of my life thinking that Jesus was disappointed with me because of my less than stellar performance.

The emptiness we feel causes our need for approval to escalate into overdrive. The intense effort we put into arriving *there* is futile. It's as if we're running with all our might on a treadmill we can't get off. No matter how hard we try, we just can't seem to get there. Failing to get off the treadmill will eventually cause us to crash. At this point, it's even possible to fall into doing things we never dreamed we would do.

This is how we begin to spiral out of control. It usually starts with sensing conviction but ignoring it. The Holy Spirit begins calling you out for something that is developing within you. But if you aren't careful, you can develop a habit of ignoring His leading over time. It's much easier to ignore the promptings of the Holy Spirit if you have continually built up a resistance to them. The unavoidable result of acting in this fashion is a hardened heart.

It's difficult to comprehend how a spiritual leader who has experienced great success in serving Jesus could suddenly get disconnected from the Holy Spirit's leading. The mistake is in thinking it happens suddenly, which is never the case. It happens progressively—even to the point that you don't know when your heart became hardened. Therefore, it is possible for God to remove His anointing from your ministry and for you to continue without even knowing it.

This is exactly what happened to Samson as he moved further and further from his purpose. He continued flirting with disaster until it caught him. After revealing to Delilah the source of his strength, he rose up to attack the Philistines as he had before, unaware that his anointing had left him. "She said, 'The Philistines are upon you, Samson!' So he awoke from his sleep, and said, 'I will go out as before, at other times, and shake myself free!' But he did not know that the LORD had departed from him" (Judges 16:20 NKJV).

I'm sure you know how Samson's story ends. His eyes were gouged out, and he became a slave who was forced to do hard labor. God did eventually restore his strength and anointing. However, the progressive nature of becoming hard-hearted ultimately contributed to his death.

I can think of nothing worse than having the Lord depart from you without you knowing it. This is the sad consequence of developing a hard heart through approval addiction.

Dan went on to say, "Any pastor who becomes addicted to the approval of people will eventually be slaughtered by their disapproval."

In other words, if we don't deal with our need for approval, our negligence can lead to the end of our ministries. It may even bring the end to our marriages or other key relationships.

The bottom line is that a need for approval is a valid need. It's when we let it consume and control us that life can spin out of control. Consider that your need for approval is also a need for acceptance. If we don't feel accepted by the people we love and serve, how can we have that need met without destroying ourselves?

Dan shared with me that he developed a discipline he named "Thirty-Four Minutes of Acceptance," which helped him overcome approval addiction. The practice is designed to enable him to get approval every day from his heavenly Father. Anyone suffering from approval addiction can benefit greatly from following Dan's wisdom. You too can hear your heavenly Father say, "You're approved."

THIRTY-FOUR MINUTES OF ACCEPTANCE PLAN

First, set your phone, tablet, computer, or Bible to automatically show you a scripture that tells you who you are in Jesus first thing in the morning. Don't view or do anything else until you've read this encouraging passage.

Second, block the first thirty-four minutes of the day to go on a walk with God in the cool of the morning. (Although Adam and Eve walked with God in the cool of the evening [Gen. 3:8], it is probably best for the majority of us to do so first thing in the morning to avoid distractions.) This practice is also predicated on not taking any phone calls, doing any work, or viewing any form of media, including the morning news.

Third, limit what you do during your thirty-four-minute walk to meditating on the passage you read, praying in the Spirit, or listening to worship music that encourages you in the areas of approval and acceptance. As you walk with Him, spend time listening to the Father tell you that He approves of you. (Note: this is not the time to pray over your normal daily requests and such.) Use the thirty-four minutes of acceptance specifically to allow Him to lavish His approval on you.

Fourth, if you're married and/or a parent, find a way to serve your spouse and/or children immediately upon returning home. Dan serves his wife by preparing her morning coffee. I really love this point. It highlights the need to reconnect daily with the people in your life who matter most. There is no other human experience that helps me relate more to how Father God feels about me than the love and acceptance I feel for my wife, children, and grandchildren.

The goal of developing the discipline of the thirty-four minutes of acceptance is to remove the fear of failure from your life. You will know you're free when the things you feared before don't scare you anymore. The freedom you begin to experience results from knowing what it's like to be absolutely loved and cared for and free. It's so awesome to know you're loved and accepted.

THE POWER OF WORDS

My friend Sam invited me to join him on a guided fishing trip for striped bass on Lake Cumberland in Kentucky. His uncle, who is known as a top-notch guide, would serve as our host. It didn't take much time at all to see that Sam's uncle was excellent at locating the fish. He knew exactly where to go and how to set up in order for us to have a successful outing. His reputation was spot-on.

I hadn't met our guide before our trip, but Sam shared some insight as to how his uncle is wired. He is an ex-military man who went on several tours of duty including tours in Vietnam and Iraq. Being a child of the sixties contributed to his straightforward personality. I learned within a few minutes of meeting him that I need not ask him what he thinks if I really don't want to know the answer. I made every effort just to lie low and keep my opinions to myself.

In all honesty, I didn't want to go on the trip. It wasn't that I didn't want the time with my friend. I enjoy his conversation and company. It certainly wasn't that I do not enjoy fishing. Everyone who knows me understands that isn't the case at all. I love to fish—at least when they are biting. But I did have a great deal of work to get done and some tight deadlines to meet.

The real reason I didn't want to go was that we had to drive six hours to get there. Then, after getting up at four o'clock the next morning and fishing until noon, we were going to load up and head right back home. I don't really enjoy long road trips anymore. Regardless of my reason for not wanting to go, I did join Sam on the trip.

On a guided fishing trip, the guide does everything for you. He provides everything you need, from fishing tackle to bait to the meals you eat. He puts the bait on your hook and lowers the line into the water for you. He even sets it to the proper depth. All you actually do is reel the fish in once it has hooked itself. Even after you land the fish in the boat, the guide takes the fish off your hook, rebaits it, and puts the line back in the water so you can catch another. When our trip was complete, our guide even cleaned our fish for us. It's the best way in the world to fish.

A guided experience usually includes a short instructional speech that contains a few essentials for a day of fishing. Our speech included the following instructions:

1. Once the fish is hooked, let the rod bend continuously before you start reeling.
2. Make sure you start reeling before taking the rod out of the rod holder.
3. Place your left hand on the grip above the reel when you take the rod out of its holder.
4. Place the butt of the rod below your belt.
5. Point your rod tip up in the air at the eleven o'clock position.
6. Most important, keep reeling in the line at *all* times. You must not stop. (Stopping almost guarantees that a hooked fish will escape.)

Simple instructions. Right? I thought I shouldn't have a problem with this. After all, I'm a good listener. Six things to remember. No big deal. So now, bring on the fish.

Just let me say, these six instructions are much easier to follow when you aren't catching fish. As you can probably imagine, as soon as the first fish was on the line, I forgot everything our guide said. The rush of hooking up a running striper will cause you to panic. Which is exactly what I did. I had a really large fish on my hook but lost him because I stopped reeling for a split second, which was long enough for him to spit the hook out. Boy, did I get an earful from the guide. But eventually I got the process down and landed several really nice fish. Until …

The fishing action slowed to a crawl for about an hour when all of a sudden—*bam!*—my rod tip bent toward the water, and everyone could tell I had a big one on the line. So I followed the process … I reeled as fast as I could with all my might. By now, after catching several other fish, my muscles were sore and I was fatigued. Suddenly a ten-pound monster broke the surface about twenty yards from our boat. That's when the intensity went into warp speed. Everyone was excited, shifting positions, and yelling. I was trying my absolute best to land the fish that I could now see. My arm and shoulder were killing me along with my stomach, where I had wrongly placed the butt of the rod. It was almost impossible for me to wind the reel because of the pressure that big fish created. Meanwhile, our guide continued to yell at me to keep reeling.

In an effort to keep me from losing the awesome catch, he soon moved into a level of *encouragement* that I hadn't experienced since high school football. He was trying to motivate me to keep reeling. I was already pouring everything I had into it. Truthfully, my strength was so zapped at that point that I began questioning whether I had what it would take to land that fish.

Then, out of nowhere, it happened. At the precise moment I was questioning my strength, a voice erupted from the depths of my soul. *Dude, you are such a big loser. I can't believe you're performing so poorly. Anybody could land this fish. C'mon, Dale.* I began to feel emotions I hadn't experienced in decades.

The guide's efforts at *encouragement* had inadvertently caused me to start thinking I was a worthless piece of nothing. I felt so defeated that I visualized myself as that seven-year-old kid again—the one who couldn't do anything right. I kept wondering as I fought the fish, *Why is this happening in me?*

The good news in that moment was that I landed the big fish. My friend and the guide were really happy for me. They were completely unaware that I wanted to get off the boat and run far away. You see, in that moment of intense battle, the words of an authority figure I respected caused feelings of inferiority from the past to resurface in my mind and nearly destroyed me. At that point, fishing was no longer fun because I felt like a loser. My physical struggle to land that fish unlocked some powerful internal pain. I'll never forget how worthless I felt because I struggled in my performance. Those words cut me to the core.

WORDS SAID OVER US, TO US, OR ABOUT US—WHETHER INTENTIONAL OR CASUAL—CAN CRIPPLE OUR ABILITY TO LEAD.

I hadn't experienced feelings like that in many, many years. However, as I thought through what happened in me, I realized that Jesus wanted me to go through this experience in order to relate to many of you who are dealing with a similar issue. Instead of dealing with a lack of affirmation, you may be dealing with the consequences of the negative things that have been deposited in the depths of your soul through discouraging words. The Lord took me out of my normal routine and allowed me to experience the pain that many of you live with every day. He allowed me to lose the joy of fishing for a few moments to help me understand why you have lost the joy of being a fisher of people, as Jesus called you to be.

For many of us, our issue isn't that we haven't received enough affirming words. The opposite is true. We have to fight to overcome a lifetime of negative words spoken over us, to us, and about us. Instead of seeking a fill-up, we try to *empty* our emotional tanks.

The Bible teaches that the impact of spoken words actually becomes a part of our lives: "The words of a gossip are like choice morsels; they go down to the inmost parts" (Prov. 18:8 NIV). This is true whether the words are positive or negative. You and I are products of what has been spoken over us throughout our lifetimes. We embody those words in some fashion.

You will never walk in the freedom necessary to build a sustained ministry as long as you believe the negative things spoken over you. But what was said isn't the issue. *The issue arises out of you believing what was said.* Those words have caused you to accept a wrong understanding of who you are as a leader. Those words have limited your belief in what Jesus can do through you. In a sense, the misconception you have bought into has caused you to take yourself out of the battle. This wrong understanding has led you to choose to stay on the sidelines instead of allowing God to work through you as you actively engage.

My encounter with damaging words came without warning on that fishing boat. I was caught completely off guard with what I felt about myself in that moment. It was like a dam that had been holding back a torrent of emotion for years finally broke.

Friend, if your past includes years of ridicule, discouraging comments, and being told you aren't good enough, I can certainly understand why you thought you'd be there by now. Even as I write this, my eyes are filled with tears and my heart breaks for you. How can you ever have joy in the journey when the authority figures in your life have spoken so much pain into your soul?

Perhaps the words spoken into your soul continue speaking to you today. The fact is that your father, mother, coach, teacher, boss, pastor, or other authority figure thought he or she was helping you reach your potential. He thought he was making you a better person. She was probably just doing to you what had been done to her. Whatever the reasoning of those people, they most likely have no idea the effect their words had on you.

Words said over us, to us, or about us—whether intentional or casual—can cripple our ability to lead. Once a difficult situation challenges our ability to perform, those feelings that accompanied earlier harsh comments surface. It is only natural to want to empty the negative reserves you have accumulated in your emotional tank. Why wouldn't you want those things out of your soul?

In case this has hit home with you, I'd like to share the most powerful way I know to help you be free from the effect of those words: you have to forgive. Not for the offender but for yourself. It won't be easy. But it is necessary.

A practical way to do this is to write a letter to the person who hurt you. Find a place where you can be totally alone. Don't hold back anything, and don't stop writing until it's all out—every bad memory and every harmful word. Once you've written the letter, speak out loud to the person who is not there. Say aloud that you forgive him or her. Pray, cry, scream, and do whatever is necessary until you feel release within you. Then, after you have experienced your breakthrough, burn the letter.

IT'S NOT ENOUGH SIMPLY TO PURGE YOURSELF OF THE OLD. IT'S IMPERATIVE THAT YOU ALSO REPLACE THE BAD WITH GOOD.

I have one major caution as you begin to empty your emotional tank of all the impurities deposited in you. It's not enough simply to purge yourself of the old. It's imperative that you also replace the bad with good. You will never experience the wholeness you desire only by emptying yourself out. You must replenish yourself by pouring in the right things.

A great place to start is by letting go of your *if onlys*.

IF ONLY ...

Let's revisit Jesus' relationship with His good friend Mary for a moment. An even-greater revelation came after He commended her for choosing what is essential. We know that Mary, along with Martha and her brother, Lazarus, spent time with Jesus on several occasions. I'm certain He gave them an exciting personal narrative of many of the encounters He had with people along the way.

No doubt at some point He shared the story of how a prostitute entered a Pharisee's house and washed Jesus' feet with her tears (Luke 7:36–50). She then dried His feet with her hair and poured perfume from an alabaster bottle on them. I can only imagine how He delighted in telling them how He forgave her sins because of her faith.

The vibe I get from Scripture is that Mary, Martha, and Lazarus were not lower class. It appears that they did just fine economically. However, the prostitute was obviously from the other side of the tracks. Her willingness to pour out a bottle of expensive perfume must have caused Mary to take notice of her faith. The story seems to emphasize that a person who has been forgiven more will tend to love more.

I'm sure Mary was confident in her relationship with Jesus. After all, she was the one Jesus described as having chosen what is essential. However, she later experienced something that would shake her faith to the core.

We read in John 11 that Lazarus became sick—even to the point of death. So Mary and Martha sent word to Jesus, asking Him to come and heal their brother and His friend. I'm sure their confidence was strong that everything would be all right as soon as Jesus got there. I imagine they witnessed Jesus perform miracles as they spent time with Him. And the stories they would have heard … Amazing. Their confidence was unshakable at this point. However, to their dismay, Jesus delayed His return to their home, and Lazarus died before He arrived.

When Martha heard that Jesus was near, she went out to meet Him on the road. Even though she was grieving and filled with questions, she still did her best to trust Him. Mary, however, did not go out to meet Jesus. I believe her reason was much more than grief. I think she was hurt and angry and extremely disappointed in Him because He hadn't shown up in time to save her brother.

Think about it. Their family was tight with Jesus. She could certainly expect Him to show up after they had been so faithful. Right? But He didn't show. Jesus failed to meet her expectations. But because they were so close, Mary knew He would know exactly how she felt as soon as He saw her.

It was only after Martha returned to let her know He wanted to see her that Mary went out to meet Him. Let's pick up the story here: "Jesus had not yet entered the town but was still at the place where Martha had met him. When her sympathizing Jewish friends saw Mary run off, they followed her, thinking she was on her way to the tomb to weep there. Mary came to where Jesus was waiting and fell at his feet, saying, 'Master, if only you had been here, my brother would not have died'" (vv. 30–32).

Have you ever had a moment in which you confidently knew that Jesus was going to come through for you? Your expectations were at an all-time high. After all, you have a track record of choosing what is *essential*, just as Mary did. You have been faithfully serving Him for years. I mean, look at the fruit you have produced. But the moment passed, and you were left wondering where He was. *If only* You *had been here, then* _____ *would not have happened.* (Fill in the blank with your own experience.)

The years that add up to thinking you would be there by now are filled with the *if only*s of disappointed expectations.

SERVE, SIT, OR SURRENDER

The narrative goes on to show how Jesus raised Lazarus from the dead after he had been in the grave for four days. Wow. Jesus truly is the resurrection and the life. The raising of Lazarus became the catalyst for the masses wanting to anoint Jesus as their king. Momentum started building after such a great miracle and led to a triumphant entry into the city for the week of Passover (John 12:12–18). However, after some serious soul searching, Mary experienced a completely different level in her relationship with Jesus.

This scene shows how Mary responded to her if-only a few days later: "Six days before Passover, Jesus entered Bethany where Lazarus, so recently raised from the dead, was living. Lazarus and his sisters invited Jesus to dinner at their home. Martha served. Lazarus was one of those sitting at the table with them. Mary came in with a jar of very expensive aromatic oils, anointed and massaged Jesus' feet, and then wiped them with her hair. The fragrance of the oils filled the house" (vv. 1–3).

I love this setting for so many reasons. They all gathered in the house for another meal with Jesus. You would expect there to be a new dynamic in their relationship after Jesus raised Lazarus from the dead, wouldn't you? However, some things stayed the same and some things dramatically changed.

Simply put, Martha was laboring; Lazarus was living; Mary was lavishing.

Martha returned to her default of *serving*. Don't misunderstand Martha. She was obviously wired with a gift of hospitality. However, it seems to me that serving would not have been as important in that moment. After all, her brother, who had been dead, was sitting at the table with Jesus. Wouldn't you think she would want to be in on that table talk?

Lazarus joined others at the table in order to *sit* with Jesus. Lazarus had been dead for four days. The man who was dead was now alive again. I think he learned the value of sitting from observing Mary's earlier example. It seems only natural that he would want to stay close to the Source of life.

Mary responded by worshipping Jesus through an act of complete *surrender*. There is so much more to what Mary did in that moment than meets the eye. She massaged His feet while pouring out very expensive perfume and dried them with her hair just like the prostitute she had heard about. Something obviously happened in Mary after she saw her brother raised from the dead. I'm convinced she began to see Jesus in a different way.

A resurrection will cause you to step back and process. In the days following Lazarus's resurrection, I believe Mary spent a lot of time reflecting on what had happened. At some point she began to understand the prostitute's act of worship as well. Mary probably thought, *What did this woman understand that gave her the courage to barge into a Pharisee's house and approach Jesus? What led her to an act of such complete surrender?* Mary realized that the woman saw Jesus by faith with greater clarity than Mary had been able to see Him.

Reflecting on her if-only encounter caused her to question everything about her relationship with Jesus and gave her a deeper revelation of His amazing love. Is it possible that your disappointment about not being there by now comes out of thinking, *If only He had been here by now?*

IS IT POSSIBLE THAT YOUR DISAPPOINTMENT ABOUT NOT BEING THERE BY NOW COMES OUT OF THINKING, *IF ONLY HE HAD BEEN HERE BY NOW?*

Mary actually went a step further than the prostitute in her act of surrendered worship. She poured out an entire jar of oil compared with the prostitute, who poured out only a bottle of oil. Her sacrifice was worth a year's wages, according to Judas. She was not trying to outperform the other woman. She was just so grateful for the revelation she had experienced that she expressed her faith in a lavish way.

Maybe, like Mary, you have reached a point in your ministry that compels you to act in a bold way. The time has come to lavish your love on Jesus by faith.

Ministry is progressive. You enter with a *serving* mentality. The next level is to choose what's essential by learning the value of *sitting* with Jesus. However, the place you ultimately want to live the rest of your days is the place of *surrender*. You will know you're there when you let go of the if-onlys because you realize He has always been there.

DIGGING DEEPER

1. Have your years of faithful service led you to serve, sit, or surrender? What would true surrender look like in your life?
2. What makes you think it might be time for a resurrection of your ministry? Instead of focusing on the if-onlys of the past, get in a quiet place today and begin pouring out your heart to Jesus.
3. Traveling forward while looking backward always causes us to wind up in the ditch. How might a continuous posture of surrender help shift your focus and increase your faith?
4. If you decided to pray for a resurrection and expected it to happen, how do you think your ministry would change?

5

TRANSITION

Courage is a nonnegotiable quality for the next generation leader.

—Andy Stanley, *Next Generation Leader*

I'm constantly amazed at how much people dislike change. You've probably discovered, as I have, that this is especially true in the church. We seldom hear stories of congregations that celebrate the transition from doing church status quo to eagerly embracing a new way of operating. In truth, effective transition usually happens through great leadership.

My hope for you is that you are sensing newfound courage to lead your ministry through a positive transition to increase its impact in the surrounding community. I believe Jesus is raising up transitional leaders to help our churches move into the next season of great harvest. You can't force people to change, but you can lovingly walk them through it.

In this chapter I want to help you understand that you are not in this alone. I also want to paint a clear picture of whom we are trying to reach. I pray that Jesus gives you special favor to enlighten those you lead about what's really at stake.

YOU ARE NOT ALONE

I had an epiphany a few years ago when I began to understand that my discouragement and shame were part of an elaborate scheme. I realized the scheme was designed to keep me from fulfilling Jesus' purpose for my life. As a fellow leader, you are included in this scheme too. In fact, I believe your induction came at the moment you accepted the call to serve in ministry. As author of this scheme, Satan's goal has always been to destroy your passion, your vision, and your purpose in ministry. If he can't take you out of this world, then he wants to thwart your purpose and undermine your ability to make a difference.

Actually, there is more to the scheme than creating discouraged pastors and other leaders. Much more. The endgame for Satan isn't just to derail you. He wants to destroy your entire ministry effectiveness. He understands he can do even more damage to God's kingdom if he can remove, or at least render ineffective, the leaders in the church. While it is true that he hates everyone, his attack on pastors and other leaders has a greater impact.

Don't miss this, my friend. Satan's primary goal is to destroy the church. When a frontal assault on the leaders doesn't work, he patiently waits for them to allow discouragement and shame to set in. It may take some time, but he knows this plan will have serious consequences. One thing worse than a discouraged leader who thinks he or she should be there by now is an entire church body that feels that way.

There are thousands of churches in our world that focus more on what God did in the past than what He is doing today. As time goes on, they lose any awareness of the next generation. In fact, they often become critical because these young people don't seem to know God or understand how He once moved in their church. In their criticism, they unknowingly create barriers that make it difficult for any outsider to become a part of the church.

This attitude plays right into Satan's plan, because his goal is to destroy the church's ability to reach the next generation.

SATAN'S PRIMARY GOAL IS TO DESTROY THE CHURCH.

Anyone with cultural awareness can see that things are changing at an unprecedented rate today. Throughout America and around the world, it appears that the influence of the local church is at an all-time low. Our inability to reach the next generation will have devastating consequences if we don't wake up.

As a teenager growing up in the seventies, I often heard that more than 90 percent of all salvations happen before people turn eighteen. In reality, according to Barna Group, adults age nineteen and over have just a 6 percent probability of becoming Christians.[10]

Reaching the next generation can no longer be left up to chance. It has got to be a top priority for our churches. Unfortunately, this becomes increasingly unlikely when the most urgent focus of so many churches is survival. Continuing in survival mode will almost certainly prevent a church from influencing the next generation. It's easier to overlook young people because they don't have the resources needed to pay the bills, which are increasingly hard to cover. When we're in survival mode, we tend to overlook the far-reaching implications of failing to reach and disciple our young people.

For those who lead, the added pressure to survive can be overwhelming at times. It can cause you to feel as though you've been singled out and attacked as a leader. However, this really is not the case at all. *You* haven't been singled out. *We* have been attacked—by a real Enemy with a real goal of destroying the church's ability to reach the young.

I believe with all my heart that the discouragement, disenfranchisement, and defeat we experience are part of a thinly veiled attempt to thwart our ability to reach our youth. The next generation is depending on pastors and other leaders like you and me to stand in the gap for them.

THE NEXT GENERATION IS DEPENDING ON PASTORS AND

OTHER LEADERS LIKE YOU AND ME TO STAND IN THE GAP

FOR THEM.

Please take a moment right now and make this statement out loud: "I'm not alone." Make it a focus of prayer. Ask Jesus to open your heart to see that future generations are at stake here. Then let's learn from those who have gone before us the incredible difference one leader can make with a heart for the next generation.

GENERATIONAL TRANSFER

I respect so many great leaders in the church today. One such leader is Willie George, the founding pastor of Church on the Move in Tulsa, Oklahoma. I have been encouraged by watching how he developed from a children's ministry leader named Gospel Bill in the eighties into a seasoned leader with so much wisdom and influence. Church on the Move has always made strong children's and youth ministry a major focus. Although Pastor Willie recently turned the pastoral reins over to his son and daughter-in-law Whit and Heather George, he has modeled for us the proper way to define success in ministry. Success isn't about what I accomplish today. Success is best demonstrated by raising up a successor. Ongoing success requires that the successor also raise up successors. Without this process, the ministry will cease as the current generation dies and the next generation comes along.

Throughout the Bible we can see how the people of God didn't do such a great job of creating successors. Pastor Willie said, "There is no such thing in the Bible as a guaranteed generational transfer." In other words, just because the current generation is going strong by impacting the culture and community for Jesus doesn't mean that the next generation will do the same. Pastor Willie taught that we must be intentional about raising up the next generation through our mission, our strategy, and even our budgeting.

I have observed how congregations that aren't intentionally led to focus on reaching the next generation will always structure their ministries in a way that best suits them. Simply put, people tend to do what benefits them the most at the time. It becomes easier for a discouraged leader to acquiesce to the will of the people than to challenge them to think beyond meeting their own needs.

Although these folks may get their way at the moment, seldom do they realize the long-term effect of failing to reach the next generation. Eventually the people realize there are no longer any young families around. And more often than not, they have waited too long to bring about lasting change.

SUCCESS IS BEST DEMONSTRATED BY RAISING UP A SUCCESSOR.

In Joshua 24 we see that Joshua's season of leading God's people was coming to an end. He challenged the Israelites to stay focused and remain faithful in their commitment to God. He reminded them time and time again that their children's futures were at stake should they choose to worship foreign gods. With his declaration that his family would always serve God, he was calling them to make the same commitment. Joshua was a leader who kept the standard high throughout his lifetime. His influence on the other leaders also helped many of them stay faithful, even after his death.

But then look at Judges 2:10: "Another generation grew up that didn't know anything of GOD or the work he had done for Israel." Wait a minute. What happened? How did the narrative change so drastically? It went from the leaders left behind after Joshua's death being worshippers of God to the next generation not knowing anything of God or the work He had done for Israel. How could that have happened?

Somewhere along the way, they failed to pass on what they knew about God—so much so that we find a generation raised by the people of God yet who knew nothing about Him or the works He had done for their parents.

A pattern recurs throughout Judges. The people walk with God. Then they are led astray by foreign influences and rebel against God. They end up in bondage and repent. God rescues and restores them, and then they repeat the cycle. The lack of consistent leadership gives rise to the conclusion of the book of Judges: "At that time there was no king in Israel. People did whatever they felt like doing" (21:25). My guess is that some of the leaders failed to uphold the standards Joshua held.

Successful generational transfer is as much caught as it is taught. It is impossible to place too much value on the priority of learning God's Word. Everybody knows this is true. However, there is more to discipleship than the academic study of Scripture. It also has to be modeled in our daily lives. A courageous leader is one who becomes an agent of change by holding high standards, even in the face of congregational disagreement.

BECOMING AN AGENT OF CHANGE

Research continues to reveal that most pastors today don't feel adequately trained to lead their churches. We're also faced with a jolting realization that many of the people in our churches have no desire to be led.

Knowing this makes it difficult to accept our role as leaders and agents of change. Sometimes part of our discouragement comes from the challenge of embracing the responsibility to lead. Often we've been leading at a certain level, but we've slammed into a barrier that stops us in our tracks. This happened to me at one point in my leadership.

Our church had experienced years of steady growth and an encouraging rate of conversions for our size. We had recruited well and established a level of leadership responsibilities that people took seriously. We had positive momentum and a clear vision to reach the unchurched and the dechurched. However, my unwillingness to confront some issues within the church eventually derailed us. Plain and simple, I chickened out. And I knew I was chickening out. I allowed myself to make excuses to avoid dealing with the problems.

Here are a few of the excuses I used to avoid confrontation:

- People will leave the church if I confront the problems.
- I'm too young to confront people older than me.
- Confronting the problems will stop our momentum.
- Most people aren't even aware we have problems. Confronting them openly will reveal the problems to the congregation and community.
- Leaders who disagree with me will quit or leave.
- Given enough time, maybe the problems will resolve themselves.
- Maybe I can create enough good activity to overshadow the problems and reduce their effect on the church.

Do any of those sound familiar to you?

As you can see, I worked overtime to avoid confronting our problems. Eventually they all blew up in my face. Without exception, every scenario I tried to avoid ended up materializing anyway. The consequences I tried to prevent through avoidance actually became a direct result of my avoidance.

What about you, my friend? Are you spending more energy developing excuses for not confronting the problems than you would spend if you did confront them? I can obviously relate if this describes you. Unknown consequences intimidated me so much that I backed myself into a corner. Yet it was in that corner that the spotlight shone the brightest on me. I had failed to comprehend that my excuses were an attempt to divert attention from my leadership weaknesses. Yet, to my horror, they exposed my leadership insecurities for all to see.

AS LEADERS, PARENTS, AND GRANDPARENTS, WE MUST BE COMMITTED TO MAKING SURE THAT FUTURE GENERATIONS NOT ONLY KNOW *ABOUT* GOD BUT ALSO ACTUALLY *KNOW* GOD.

In order to become an agent of change, you must first examine the standards you've upheld in your church. Then you must be willing to raise them regardless of the backlash you may receive from church members who want to maintain the status quo. You also must surrender your fears of what others will say or do and trust that God will reward your integrity.

The truth is, your church needs you to step up and lead whether they know it or not. It is also true that you can't just go and change the structure of your church this week. In fact, the structure presented in Scripture is heresy to thousands and thousands of churches. But you've got to start somewhere. There has got to be a major overhaul of how we do church if we have any hope of reversing the current tide of church decline and death. And here is the good news, Pastor … You get to lead this overhaul.

As leaders, parents, and grandparents, we must be committed to making sure that future generations not only know *about* God but also actually *know* God. The transition from maintaining the same old routine to being willing to change requires amazing leadership. With so much at stake, I hope you are sensing a new courage and boldness to help your church transition in the coming days.

DIGGING DEEPER

1. What areas of your leadership need to be addressed for you to become a transitional leader?

2. What specific attacks has the Enemy used to discourage you from being a transitional leader? Name some ways your ministry can be more effective at connecting with the next generation. Think outside the normal church programs as you consider this.

3. What ideas can you explore with the older saints in your church to help them see the need to reach the next generation?

4. What areas do you tend to avoid approaching because of your fear of confrontation? Present each of these to the Lord in prayer over the next thirty days by writing them down individually. Ask Him to help you overcome this fear.

6

TRANSFORMATION

If we are to better the future, we must disturb the present.

—Catherine Booth, *For God Alone*

Obviously, it would be much easier to continue leading our churches and ministries in the same direction we have always led them. However, I hope by now you are willing to embrace the challenge of taking the road less traveled. It doesn't take an expert to realize that maintaining our current trajectory will result in dire consequences for future generations. In reality, our culture simply can't afford for us to lose.

When I reflect on how I arrived at thinking I would be there by now, I realize I was more focused on transportation than transformation. Here's what I mean.

Transformation is all about being changed from the inside out, as Romans 12:2 describes. Transformation takes place as we renew our minds with God's Word. The Greek word for "transform" is *metamorphoō*. Our English word *metamorphosis*, often used to describe the process of a caterpillar changing into a butterfly, comes from it. HELPS Word Studies defines the root word *morphoō* this way: "changing *form* in keeping with inner reality."[11]

I love that! The transformation that many of our churches need to experience is to change their form while keeping their inner reality. In other words, it's possible to embrace a new format and still retain all the depth and character of our deeply held beliefs.

Transportation is all about how we look as we proceed on the journey. At some point along the way, I began to focus on the image I wanted everyone to see. I had inverted the process from inside out to outside in. Therefore, instead of allowing God to patiently transform me, I fixated on my abilities and performance.

My fixation with transportation eventually stopped my progress. I reached the point at which I had no energy left to put into my performance. Shame, stress, guilt, and the pressure I was living under each day had me feeling like a failure. When that happened, I lost sight of why I was doing what I did and whom I was trying to serve.

WHEN I REFLECT ON HOW I ARRIVED AT THINKING I WOULD BE THERE BY NOW, I REALIZE I WAS MORE FOCUSED ON TRANSPORTATION THAN TRANSFORMATION.

Thank God, I finally came to an understanding that I needed to focus on Jesus' ability to transform me. After that happened, how I looked didn't matter anymore. I soon discovered that a transformed leader is much more likely to help transform the organization he or she leads.

STANDING IN THE GAP

David was described as "a man after [God's] own heart" (1 Sam. 13:14; Acts 13:22 NIV). He certainly experienced a lot of ups and downs throughout his life. However, he didn't allow the responsibilities of being king or the difficulties he often faced to squelch his passion for the next generation. He said, "Even when I am old and gray, do not forsake me, my God, till I declare your power to the next generation, your mighty acts to all who are to come" (Ps. 71:18 NIV).

Although David knew he was getting up in years, he didn't want his life to end without letting the next generation know who God was and what He had done. King David could have had anything on his agenda in his final years. Yet the next generation was an important priority to him. My heart is so moved when I meet older saints who understand the need to invest in the next generation.

I don't know of any biblical leader who had a more daunting task of leading the next generation than Moses. Think about it for a minute. At forty years old he killed an Egyptian who was being cruel to an Israelite slave. Even then, Moses sensed his own calling to be a deliverer of God's people. Unfortunately, he went about it the wrong way and had to flee for his life (Ex. 2:11–15).

There in the desert, God transformed him over the next forty years, equipping him with the tools necessary to eventually save an entire generation in the wilderness. When Moses was eighty years old, God appeared to him in a burning bush and sent him back to Egypt to deliver His people. There Moses confronted Pharaoh. Led the people out of Egypt. Crossed the Red Sea (Ex. 3–14). And at the brink of entering the Promised Land, the people rebelled against God and refused to take the land. Are you kidding me?

Moses sent twelve of his best men to investigate the land. They returned from inspecting the Promised Land and reported to Moses. You may remember how Joshua and Caleb were ready to take possession of the land immediately—land, by the way, that God had already promised to His people. However, the other ten spies disagreed so much that they sowed unbelief throughout the entire camp. The people rose up against Moses and insisted on returning to the bondage of Egypt. They even went so far as to say that it would be better to raise their children in slavery than to die in the desert (Num. 13:1—14:4).

God was so disappointed with their rebellion that He declared that, because of their unbelief, no one over the age of nineteen would enter the Promised Land (14:28–29). The people then wandered in the desert for forty years as God used Moses to transform the next generation into people who would believe what He had promised. God used the leadership of Moses to save an entire generation whose parents had chosen to rebel against Him.

Moses's leadership, along with Joshua's, helped sustain them in the years of wandering and prepared them to take possession of the promises of God. It's impossible to place enough value on a leader who stands in the gap for the next generation.

Have you ever thought about what that next generation experienced in the desert over those forty years? There were some really good things. But there were also some difficult things.

Here are a few that come to mind.

Good Things

God's Provision. He nourished them with manna and water from a rock. Also, their clothes and shoes never wore out (Deut. 8:15–16; 29:5).

God's Direction. God continued to meet with Moses and give him direction.

God's Protection. None of their enemies were allowed to wipe them out during this time.

Difficult Things

Disillusionment. The distance to the Promised Land should have taken only a few days to cover. The Israelites basically walked in circles for forty years.

Discouragement. It wasn't their fault they were stuck in the desert. Their parents and grandparents were responsible for their fate. They must have felt like they were being unfairly punished.

Death. Most speakers rarely discuss this aspect of wandering in the desert for forty years.

Remember how God declared that none of the unbelieving parents would enter the Promised Land? In other words, they would die in the desert. Exodus 12:37 tells us that there were six hundred thousand men in addition to women and children who participated in the exodus. Some estimate as many as 2.5 million people made the journey.

To illustrate this, let's do some simple math:

Number of men during the exodus: 600,000

Estimated number of women during the exodus: 600,000

That number divided by 14,600 days (365 x 40 years)

Approximate number of daily funerals: 82

Let this sink in. Although the next generation had the Promised Land to look forward to, each day of the journey was filled with burying their parents because of their unbelief.

What you and I deal with in today's church is hard. I understand that. But come on now—we have to agree we aren't facing this much pressure. At more than eighty years old, Moses was tasked with transforming the next generation into people who trusted God while maintaining the tension between the good things and the difficult things.

How did Moses do it? I can see three things he prioritized in his transformational leadership:

First, he cared for them.

Second, he taught them God's truths and mentored them.

Third, he raised up a next-generation leader in Joshua.

It's going to take great leadership from you and me in order to close the generational gap. Learning from Moses's example would be a great place to start. Only through intentional care, strategic teaching of the Word, and a mentoring or discipleship pathway will we be able to hand off a healthy ministry to the next generation. Being willing to embrace your role as their shepherd will make the difference between success and failure.

INCREASING CAPACITY

The importance of reaching the next generation is one discussion that always elicits a passionate response in the church. And folks don't mind sharing their opinions with you when it comes up. I believe the main source of this tension flows out of the ever-increasing generation gap.

According to Haydn Shaw's book *Generational IQ*, this is the first occurrence of having five generations alive at the same time, and we don't have the generational intelligence to handle it yet.[12] Advances in medicine and overall healthier living have resulted in an increase in the average life expectancy. When I was a teen growing up in the 1970s, a generation gap basically existed between three generations: parent and child, grandparent and parent, and grandparent and grandchild. However, in my lifetime, the gap has increased greatly as people continue to live longer. We perpetuate the tension between generations by an inability to relate to any generation different from our own.

The only way to close the generation gap is to be intentional about closing it. And whether you like it or not, God is calling you as a leader of His church to make this a priority. You simply can't keep ignoring it or using the excuse of maintaining peace to avoid it. You don't have the luxury of kicking the can to the next generation. Anything less than an all-out effort to resolve the gap guarantees perpetual ineffectiveness and eventual ministry death.

Sadly, a major contributor to the generational tension in recent years has been leaders, often younger, who have displayed arrogance by being dismissive and critical of the older generations. Some have gone so far as to be antagonistic in their communication about the traditional church. This has caused many of our senior saints to feel disrespected in today's church climate.

WE PERPETUATE THE TENSION BETWEEN GENERATIONS BY AN INABILITY TO RELATE TO ANY GENERATION DIF-FERENT FROM OUR OWN.

I was raised in a region where disrespecting your elders and talking back were not tolerated. So as we address this issue, please understand that disrespecting my elders is the last thing I would ever want to do. I realized a long time ago that everything we have in the church today was built on the shoulders of those who have gone before us.

However, it's not necessarily disrespectful to older generations to discuss the real issues. Churches are closing at alarming rates. If that's not disturbing enough, there are thousands on life support and in need of immediate change if they are to remain open. We must discuss the obstacles standing in our way. Just as renewing our minds with God's Word brings transformation, spending time discussing our problems and staying engaged until we find a solution brings transformation. The goal is to emerge from these conversations with new life, mission, and vision.

Human nature tends to lead us to always choose what is best for ourselves when given options. This behavior is easy to see in the leadership of so many of our churches today. It is understandable that we would want to continue worshipping in a style and format that we hold dear.

After all, many of the folks who make up our congregations have fond memories of the good old days.

Older generations are sincere in trying to hold on to the methods through which they came to know the Lord. Bill Gaither had such a brilliant idea when he began producing the Homecoming video series, which features many of the legends of gospel music. Those videos always stir up a special memory from my childhood when I watch them. So please understand—I get it.

SPENDING TIME DISCUSSING OUR PROBLEMS AND STAYING ENGAGED UNTIL WE FIND A SOLUTION BRINGS TRANSFORMATION.

However, my ability to get it doesn't mean the next generation gets it. It's easy to get the *methods* confused with the *message*. It may be natural to assume that the way I came into a relationship with the Lord is the norm. It may seem customary to worship the Lord the way I like to worship. However, this doesn't mean my way is the only way.

Christians naturally revert to the moments when they felt a connection with Jesus. This is true whether we're old or young. But it's a mistake to discount someone else's experience regardless of when that person had it. We typically tend to determine authenticity through the view of our own lenses.

Let me illustrate this by showing two views of the same verse of Scripture. Hebrews 13:8 says, "Jesus Christ is the same yesterday, today, and forever" (NKJV). Older generations tend to read this verse and come away with the view that older ways of relating to Jesus are what is important. They emphasize *yesterday*. Younger generations tend to read this verse and come away with the view that contemporary ways of relating to Jesus are what is important. They emphasize *today*.

Who is right, then? Would you believe they both are? The Jesus who moved in the lives of the older generation yesterday is the same Jesus who is moving in the lives of the younger generation today. And here's a news flash—He is the same Jesus who will be there for both generations tomorrow.

The issue lies in thinking the *methods* are sacred. But the *message* is sacred, not the methods. Our churches are in desperate need of a trans-formational shift in how we view what's important.

If I'm not careful, I will start using phrases such as "the good old days" and "We need an old-fashioned revival" in order to paint a picture of what God did in my life. Sometimes we can even go as far as erecting a tent in the parking lot beside our air-conditioned buildings with hopes of re-creating a revival atmosphere from the past. In most cases, nobody intends to adopt a stuck-in-the-past approach. Rather, they are sincerely remembering a past personal encounter with the Lord.

This way of reminiscing always leads us to remember what God *did* in our lives instead of focusing on what God is *doing* currently.

THE *MESSAGE* IS SACRED, NOT THE *METHODS*.

It is human nature to want to relive my own personal experiences. It's normal to want to camp around an experience. Even Peter made this suggestion to Jesus on the Mount of Transfiguration: "Lord, it is good that we are here. If you want, I will put up three tents here—one for you, one for Moses, and one for Elijah" (Matt. 17:4 NCV).

I don't blame Peter at all. I'm sure I would have wanted to camp there too. Who wouldn't want to camp with Jesus, Moses, and Elijah? The Father even spoke out loud. It really can't get any better than that. Can it?

Actually, yes, it can. And therein lies the problem. Being in relation-ship with Jesus requires daily interaction, not reflective ritual. If they had camped there, Peter would have missed out on an incredible future with

Jesus, which included preaching a message that caused thousands of people to be saved (Acts 2:14–41). I've come to realize that this same behavior is what led me to think I would be there by now. Feeling stuck in a place of failure kept me from boldly greeting Him each day to discover what new things were waiting for me. In a sense, I was as stalled in the past as many of those much older than me.

Friend, it's time to expand our faith. We must confront the comfort of resting in our unique generational characteristics. Without doing so, we will never be open to real change. Our capacity for growth and connecting with younger generations will be increased by embracing new ways of communicating the message.

Jesus addressed this issue as He confronted the reluctance of people who refused to accept the gospel because they were satisfied with the old legalistic system they had always known:

> No one ever pours new wine into old leather bags [wineskins]. Otherwise, the new wine will break the bags, the wine will spill out, and the leather bags will be ruined. New wine must be put into new leather bags. No one after drinking old wine wants new wine, because he says, "The old wine is better." (Luke 5:37–39 NCV)

Here are some enlightening parallels we can draw from His teaching in this passage:

1. **The wine is new.** The new wine needs room to expand during the transformational process (fermentation).
2. **The wineskins are new.** The containers that hold the new need the flexibility to expand.
3. **The old wineskins won't work.** Attempting to put a new, transformative process in old containers results in everything being lost.

4. New wine can only be preserved in new wineskins. Jesus removed the possibility of ignoring the need for new. In other words, we can't refuse to do things God's way and expect Him to bless our efforts.

5. Old wine tastes better. All wine connoisseurs know this. They will always choose an older vintage over a newer one.

The Message states verse 39 like this: "No one who has ever tasted fine aged wine prefers unaged wine." I'm so glad Luke included this verse at the end of this teaching. And through this Jesus gives us a great illustration of the modern church, in my opinion. So much depth and comfort come with our former experiences. The character and faithfulness expressed in our church traditions are as priceless as a bottle of wine that has been aged for decades.

The glaring issue that must be resolved is the reality that we will eventually have no wine if we enjoy only the old wine. The only way to ensure we have plenty of old wine in the future is to make sure we create plenty of new wine today.

Therefore, as leaders in the church, it is our responsibility to increase our congregations' capacity for new growth while honoring the heritage of the old. I want to challenge you to do your part to help close the widening generational gap. History teaches us that it will not shrink on its own. Only with courageous transformative leadership will our churches work to find the common ground needed to create positive solutions.

DIGGING DEEPER

1. What are the three most important areas in which the people in your organization need to transform their thinking? List practical steps to take toward a renewed understanding of your mission in each of those areas.

2. As you think about the next generation, name at least six issues they are dealing with each day due to our ever-changing culture. Take an inventory of your ministry with these issues in mind. How are you doing at answering the questions that relate to these issues?

3. Have you developed an intentional process to help the generations connect? If so, write out the steps. If not, list five things you can do to get the conversation started. (One example would be to require different age groups to be represented in your small groups. Then provide conversation starters so they can discuss how to close the generation gap.)

SECTION 3

THE FULFILLMENT OF LIVING THERE

THE LOOK OF THE FUTURE

You have probably noticed the number of high-profile ministry leaders who have either questioned the validity of Christianity or renounced their faith altogether over the last decade. While I think it's too early to call this development a trend, the rate at which it is happening is a bit alarming. Some of those leaders have even divorced their spouses and walked away from everything they once held to be true.

These are not leaders who thought they would be there by now. By today's standards, they had actually *arrived there*. The truth is, successful leaders questioning their beliefs is hardly new. Anyone who is willing to be transparent will tell you he or she has unanswered questions at times. I believe it is natural—and even healthy—to ask questions as we grow deeper in our relationship with the Lord over the years. He has never been one to shy away from hard questions.

A lot of the questions I asked had to do with my inability to build a larger ministry. I didn't question the Lord as much as I questioned myself. I developed beliefs that became walls built out of my feelings of failure. At some point these walls became a stronghold in my life. The stronghold became impenetrable as I continued to reinforce it by reminding myself of past failures.

In this last section, I intend to expose some strongholds that held me back. Maybe you will relate to them too. Remember, Satan has a strategic plan in place to keep us ineffective by reminding us that we should be there by now. It's time to shatter the strongholds and renounce the beliefs that are holding us back from being a blessing to the kingdom.

7

TRUE FREEDOM

*The worst thing that could happen is that you spend
your life trying to outrun God because you think he's
chasing you to collect what you owe—when he's really
chasing you to give you what you could never afford.*

—Kyle Idleman, *Grace Is Greater*

Are you ready for a fresh perspective on what success in your life and
ministry really looks like? I am not talking about a major overhaul. It's
possible that the only thing you need is to shift your view of your life
today. Maybe you just need a new paradigm.

Let's look at some principles that will help you shift your focus. The
time has come for you and me to trade the look that comes from a disillusioned failure complex for the look that comes from walking in success.
Whether you feel like it or not today, you have a bright future. All you
need to do is recognize and renounce the strongholds that have developed
in your life. Your breakthrough could be as close as shifting your gaze to the
possibilities instead of focusing on the problems.

WHAT WOULD YOU DO IF YOU KNEW YOU COULDN'T FAIL?

Gina and I had been traveling with our college group for three years. As that season came to a close, we weren't sure which direction to go next. Since we were in our early twenties, it seemed natural and expected that we would continue our education. So we scheduled a meeting with our pastor to seek his advice and gain some clarity. I didn't know it at the time, but the meeting with Pastor Brad would direct the trajectory of my life from that day forward.

After a few minutes of small talk, our conversation went something like this:

Pastor Brad: What do you feel you are called to do with your life?

Me: I want to minister to people.

Pastor Brad: That's too vague. What do you specifically feel called to do?

Me: I want to minister to young people ... and old people.

Pastor Brad: That's still too vague. What has God placed in your heart to do?

At that point, my blood pressure was rising and I was getting really uncomfortable. No one had ever asked me a question that required such a specific answer. I did have something in my heart that I wanted to do, but I hadn't even discussed it with Gina. I just assumed it was too outlandish to even consider.

Me (attempting to squirm out of my seat): I want to minister to everyone.

Pastor Brad: That's great, Dale. But how? If you knew you would be successful. If there were no barriers. If money was not a hindrance. *What would you do if you knew you couldn't fail?*

Me: I want to keep doing what we've been doing. I would start a music group and travel throughout the country, encouraging believers and reaching the lost. That's what I would do if I knew I couldn't fail.

Pastor Brad: Finally. You just revealed what Jesus has called you to do next. You're obviously going to deal with setbacks, problems, and barriers. But knowing what you would do if you overcome them is acknowledging what He has already placed in your heart. This is what gives you the ability to stick with it when times get tough.

That question has been my standard for measuring every opportunity that has come my way since. "What would you do if you knew you couldn't fail?"

WHAT WOULD YOU DO IF YOU KNEW YOU

COULDN'T FAIL?

Pastor Brad went on to tell us that he had always wanted to have a group based out of our church that traveled the country, encouraging believers and reaching the lost. Soon after our meeting, he brought us on staff to create this new ministry. We would go on to do hundreds of concerts over the next few years. Much of what I do today has its roots in those early days of traveling and working with so many churches.

Had I not spoken up when Pastor Brad asked that question, I would have missed the opportunity to do what I believed Jesus had called me to do. I would have buried what He had placed in my heart to do when the moment came.

It's easy to misunderstand the direct correlation between thinking and speaking. You may have a negative view of your calling and potential. Or you may hold a confident view of your calling and potential. No matter which way you think, your words tend to follow your thinking. "The mouth speaks what the heart is full of" (Matt. 12:34 NIV). Eventually your actions follow your words.

Speaking my dream in response to Pastor Brad's question wasn't something I made up in the moment. On the contrary, it was something I had meditated on for months. However, I didn't begin to see it come into existence until I spoke what I was thinking when the moment presented itself.

God taught this principle to Joshua in the most stressful of times. As he was preparing to lead the people into the Promised Land, Joshua faced an impossible situation. The challenges before him required that he carefully follow God's direction in order to bring about success. Attempting to do this on his own would guarantee certain failure.

I have identified six major issues Joshua faced:

1. **Moses was dead.** Joshua was then charged with following the greatest leader the people had ever known. Moses had brought them out of bondage and led them for forty years. No one ever wants to follow such a revered leader.
2. **The Jordan River was at flood stage.** During that time of year, it can be a mile wide in some places.
3. **Joshua's followers didn't have the best track record of following.** They had probably become more accustomed to wandering.
4. **The logistics of caring for that many people are astounding.** There were millions of people who needed to be led into the Promised Land. The daily task of coordinating food, water, and firewood alone would be overwhelming.

5. **Joshua had seen the enemy personally.** He knew what awaited them on the other side of the river. Remember, he and Caleb had been there forty years earlier. He knew about the giants in the land.
6. **The promised Messiah was supposed to come from the tribe of Judah.** Failure would mean the loss of His bloodline.

And I think I've got problems and pressure! God's instruction to Joshua about what to do next was critical. I imagine he expected God to provide something that possessed great power, like the staff He gave Moses. Joshua probably thought he'd at least get a walking cane or something similar. So he listened intently to God's instruction, expecting to hear what his powerful tool would be.

A review of Joshua 1:1–9 reveals that God's advice to Joshua was to meditate on His Word both day and night. That's it. If I were Joshua, I probably would have been thinking, *Seriously? Moses gets a staff and I'm told to meditate. Where's the power in that?*

I would have felt astonished. But my problem would have come from having a wrong understanding of the word *meditate*. It's not doing yoga or some form of mental exercise. *Meditate* actually means "to speak to yourself in a low tone of voice."[13] The key, however, is not so much *that* you speak as *what* you speak. The words you use are critical.

WHAT YOU HEAR MOST OFTEN WILL BE WHAT YOU BELIEVE MOST STRONGLY.

This is why God told Joshua, "This Book of the Law shall not depart from your mouth" (v. 8 NKJV). The meditation that God commanded was designed to build and sustain Joshua's faith as he led the people through an impossible situation. It's vital that we understand the influence the speaker has on the hearer. In this case, the speaker was Joshua himself.

Romans 10:17 says, "Faith comes by hearing, and hearing by the word of God" (NKJV). Don't miss this. Dozens of people can tell you they think you're a great leader. However, you only have to tell yourself one time that you are a failure as a leader, and you will believe you're a failure. Why is this? *Because you believe yourself more than you believe anyone else.*

This truth is why it is so important to speak God's Word over your life every day. Say what He says. Speak what He speaks. Verbalize the dream He has placed in your heart. After all, faith comes by hearing. What you hear most often will be what you believe most strongly.

Throughout the years, I have challenged many leaders with the question "What would you do if you knew you couldn't fail?" To my delight, many have accepted the challenge and have gone on to experience success. Unfortunately, though, most people answer the question with a blank stare accompanied by "I have no idea." I believe their inability to recognize the dreams in their hearts is due to the negative image they have of themselves. That negative image has most likely been reinforced by years of negative words they have spoken over themselves as well.

Pastor, your words really do matter, especially the words you speak to yourself. I doubt you would challenge the idea that others' negative words can do great damage to you, as we discussed in chapter 4. So why would this concept be any different? Don't let the Enemy dupe you into thinking that what you meditate on daily and the words you speak about yourself are insignificant or trivial. They are not.

ALLOW HIS WORD TO AWAKEN THE DREAM IN YOUR HEART.

Just as God told Joshua, He is telling you to meditate on His Word. Maybe you need to go on a "thirty-four minutes of acceptance" walk, as

Dan Lian suggested. When you begin to see yourself as Jesus sees you, you will be able to answer the question "What would you do if you knew you couldn't fail?" It's imperative that you start speaking His Word over your life today. Allow His Word to awaken the dream in your heart. You were created with a great purpose that you can still fulfill. You just need to hear yourself say so until you begin to believe this truth.

A REVELATION OF TRUE FREEDOM

Are you living in true freedom? I wonder how many of us would quickly reply yes. After all, Jesus died to provide freedom for all who would receive it. Right?

However, my life experiences have shown me that there are a lot of people who talk about living in freedom yet few who actually do. I imagine a big contributor to this is the lack of seeing others experience true freedom. A lot of people confuse salvation with freedom. After all, salvation has taken us from being spiritually dead to being born again into new life. What more could there be?

In reality, there's a lot more. I am in no way making light of the eternal impact of becoming a new creation. The fact that I'm saved and in right standing with God through the sacrifice of Jesus on the cross is the ultimate good news. But salvation is more than just having my ticket punched to heaven. It's much more than being left to figure out the day-to-day problems of life on my own.

To illustrate this point once while I was preaching, I put a line of duct tape down the center of the platform. I described the left side of the line as my life before accepting Jesus, the right side of the line as my life after accepting Jesus. For props, I put as many suitcases and containers as I could carry on the left side. I then demonstrated how most people experience salvation by carrying all the baggage from the left pre-salvation side over to the right post-salvation side. Then I stated, "If you were a lost person who accumulated a lot of baggage before conversion, then after conversion you became a saved person with baggage."

Your baggage doesn't necessarily go away at conversion. It can. But it normally doesn't. To help us eliminate our baggage, we need to engage in the focused process of working through a designed discipleship pathway. While this is true for those we minister to, it is also necessary for those of us in leadership. Years of accumulated baggage can easily cause a leader to think, *I should be there by now.*

I used to believe that freedom could be attained as I methodically removed each piece of baggage I had accumulated over the years. In a sense, I was trying to clean up my life in order to be a qualified vessel that Jesus could work through. I didn't realize that my default of relying on my performance had become the blockade that kept me from experiencing true freedom.

Back then I knew it was impossible to clean your life up enough to qualify for salvation. However, I didn't fully understand that the grace it took to save me was the same grace it took to qualify me for ministry. This grace is also necessary to sustain my ministry.

Jesus was so patient with me over the decades. He allowed me to struggle in my own performance until I finally realized I couldn't get there on my own. No matter how much I tried, my inability to remove enough baggage or do enough good works always had me running in circles. I was like the playground game of tetherball we played in elementary school. The harder I tried, the more wound up I became.

I was convinced that freedom was found by eliminating the baggage. If I could be rid of it somehow, then I could walk out of the prison that held me in bondage. However, here is the truth I missed. Any attempt to free myself was dependent on my ability. At its core, this is the same legalism displayed by the religious Pharisees in Jesus' day. They based their righteousness, or right-standing, on their ability to keep the rules and avoid sinful pitfalls.

As hard as they tried, though, they could never do it. Oddly enough, they kept adding more and more rules in order to be righteous. I realized I had allowed myself to do the same thing. The only difference was I focused on my ministry performance instead of salvation. Trying harder didn't bring freedom.

One of my all-time favorite verses is Galatians 5:1: "It is for freedom that Christ has set us free. Stand firm, then, and do not let yourselves be burdened again by a yoke of slavery" (NIV). I knew there had to be more to living a victorious Christian life than what I was experiencing. But I felt more like a slave than a leader living in the freedom of Christ. Thankfully, that was about to change.

FREEDOM IS NOT THE ABSENCE OF SOMETHING. IT IS THE PRESENCE OF SOMEONE.

When I discovered the Foundations of Freedom teaching by Bob Hamp, I thought the subject must be for someone else. (It's amazing how religious people in bondage focus on other people's baggage while ignoring their own.) However, a pivotal point in this teaching came when Bob said, "Freedom is not the absence of something. It is the presence of someone."

I wish I could say I immediately understood what he was saying. But I didn't get it at first. Yet, as I continued repeating the statement, the light finally dawned on me. I had been going about it all wrong. I had been trying to either eliminate a bad behavior or add a right behavior in my own strength. But I wasn't getting any closer to freedom.

The freedom I had been looking for wasn't based on my ability to remove more things from my life. Nor was it found in adding things. It was based on my willingness to allow Jesus access to every part of my life. I didn't mind giving Him the things I was proud of. On the other hand,

I was so ashamed to give Him the things that embarrassed me. I finally experienced a sense of approval when I released control and received acceptance. I had never felt that way in almost fifty years of being saved and thirty-five years of ministry. I knew in my heart that I am approved because of Jesus plus nothing.

How about you, my friend? Are you carrying around a load of baggage that has caused you to live in bondage? Has your inability to build a larger ministry caused you to become a performance-based leader trying to rid yourself of baggage? Or maybe it's caused you to try to add the right things. Although Paul told us that it's for freedom that Jesus has set us free, do you still believe the lies about your performance that keep you under a yoke of bondage?

If so, put down this book and take a moment to ask Jesus to tell you how He sees you. And then just listen for Him to speak. It might take a little time for you to hear His voice of love and acceptance. But wait for it. It's so worth allowing Him to set you free. When I heard His voice of love and acceptance, He completely changed my life. I am confident He will do the same for you.

A significant part of my freedom experience happened as I realized that Jesus didn't come to earth just to give us a passageway to heaven. He came to solve a specific problem. Understanding this truth will release a newfound power in your ministry that will propel you to places you've never been before.

THE PROBLEM JESUS CAME TO SOLVE

My life changed radically when I experienced the freedom of Jesus' love and acceptance. I became a sponge trying to soak up everything I could learn about freedom. The point of no return on my journey to freedom came when I was introduced to "The Problem Jesus Came to Solve" by Bob Hamp. The revelation I experienced as I watched the video over and over helped me understand how I had begun thinking I would be there by now.

I won't attempt to convey all the truths Bob unveiled in it, but I do want to give you an overview of his message. I highly recommend that you see the video for yourself.[14]

It all starts at the beginning in Genesis 1–3. As I was growing up, my basic understanding of the creation went something like this: God made Adam and Eve. He gave them a really cool garden to live in forever. But they messed up, so God got mad and kicked them out.

Sadly, a lot of people still understand the creation of Adam and Eve in a similar light. Yet there is a lot more to be understood about God's first interactions with human beings than appears on the surface.

I've always focused on the one special tree that God warned Adam and Eve not to eat from. In fact, I really didn't notice another tree highlighted in Genesis 2:9 for many years: "GOD made all kinds of trees grow from the ground, trees beautiful to look at and good to eat. The Tree-of-Life was in the middle of the garden, also the Tree-of-Knowledge-of-Good-and-Evil." For most of my life, I failed to understand the importance of the two trees mentioned in this verse. One tree had life as its focus or fruit. The other had knowledge of good and evil as its focus or fruit.

God warned Adam and Eve of the consequences of eating from the forbidden tree: "You must not eat from the tree of the knowledge of good and evil, for when you eat from it you will certainly die" (v. 17 NIV). Although they didn't drop dead immediately after the first bite of the forbidden fruit, they did die immediately spiritually. And in the moment that God dealt with them, He actually prophesied to the serpent that Jesus would come: "I will put enmity between you and the woman, and between your seed and her Seed; He shall bruise your head, and you shall bruise His heel" (3:15 NKJV). God announced His redemption plan in that moment. Eve's Seed would solve the problem created by their disobedience.

When asked why Jesus came to earth, most people say He came to pay the penalty for our sins. While this is certainly true, if we observe how Jesus often spoke of Himself, we begin to understand that He saw His purpose in an even broader light. Jesus taught us that the reason He came to earth was to solve the big problem rooted in Genesis. He came to give us life (John 10:10; 11:25; 14:6).

JESUS DID NOT COME TO HELP BAD PEOPLE BEHAVE (OR PERFORM) BETTER. HE CAME TO MAKE DEAD PEOPLE ALIVE.

Remember, there were two trees in the garden. The Tree of the Knowledge of Good and Evil. And the Tree of Life. This fact is essential to understanding how we begin to think we should be there by now. When our entire focus in life is on the knowledge of good and evil, we get hung up on our performance instead of connecting to the Source of life. Jesus didn't come to provide rules for us to follow. Not at all. He came to restore to us the life we lost in the garden when Adam and Eve chose knowledge over life. Jesus did not come to help bad people behave (or perform) better. He came to make dead people alive.

Let this truth sink in. When you truly understand that Jesus didn't come just to help you behave or perform correctly, it will change everything for you and your ministry. All of my life could best be described as an effort to get from the tree limb of evil onto a tree limb of good based on my knowledge of good and evil. However, He didn't give His life in order for you and me to do "better." He gave His life in order to restore life to us who were spiritually dead. That's the problem He came to solve.

As you mull this concept over, which tree do you identify with? Again, the point I am trying to make has nothing to do with your salvation. But it has everything to do with your freedom.

I think it's fair to say that the majority of Christian people I have known throughout my life are not usually joyful. Joy is an obvious fruit of living in freedom. This observation also goes for people I've known in ministry. Ouch. It's as if they are always burdened by falling short of their own expectations.

You may have had a much different experience than I have. Maybe you have been surrounded by joyful Christians. However, since you're reading this book, I'm thinking you've made a similar observation. I believe that one of the biggest hindrances keeping lost people from accepting Christ is the lack of true freedom and joy they see in many of our lives.

This problem is magnified when they see a Christian leader who is obviously bound up. We often talk about joy, but our teaching has little impact when it's not backed up by our countenances. Remember, joy doesn't flow out of performance. Joy is a fruit of the Holy Spirit's work in our lives. We are supernaturally filled with joy when we embrace the freedom that comes from being made spiritually alive in Jesus.

JOY DOESN'T FLOW OUT OF PERFORMANCE. JOY IS A FRUIT OF THE HOLY SPIRIT'S WORK IN OUR LIVES.

Do you tend to compare your good deeds and your bad deeds? Do you keep a record of your accomplishments each day that determines how you view yourself? Are you constantly striving to jump from the limb of the knowledge of evil to the limb of the knowledge of good? I can promise from my experience that you don't want to continue living this way. It eventually wears you out.

I am so thankful to finally understand the concept of doing ministry *from* Jesus instead of *for* Jesus. Remember in the Lord's Prayer when Jesus said, "Your kingdom come. Your will be done on earth as it is in heaven" (Matt. 6:10 NKJV)? How does God get what is happening in heaven to happen here on earth? He does it through His people, especially through His leaders.

Is it time for you to change trees? Let go of the weight of keeping score of your performance. Start today by connecting to the Source of life, who actually wants to establish His kingdom through you. Now is the time in your ministry to embrace His power, purpose, and plan to expand His kingdom right where you are today. He will do it if you are willing to shift your focus to the appropriate tree.

DIGGING DEEPER

1. What is your baggage composed of? Has it led you to become a performance-based leader? If so, list the ways it's manifesting itself in your life. What lies about your performance are keeping you under a yoke of bondage? Be specific.
2. Which tree in the garden of Eden do you identify with most often? Make a list of ways to compare the differences between leading your ministry through life and leading it through knowledge.
3. In what ways do you compare your good deeds with your bad deeds? How do you keep a mental record of your accomplishments each day that determines how you view yourself?
4. List some practical ways you can shift your focus from being performance motivated to being filled with life.

8

THINKING IT THROUGH

Too many of us are not living our dreams, because we are living our fears.

—Les Brown

Life's hardest lessons have a way of appearing during isolation. For example, you may feel stalled today because you serve in a rural setting where the potential for growth isn't realistic because of the miles that separate one town from another. Or you could even be struggling in a large city, feeling alone while surrounded by thousands of people. Maybe you've been in the same area for years, but the community around you has changed completely, and now you feel like an alien. Trying to stay the course while in obscurity is difficult. And dangerous.

Looking back, I can see two things that affected me a lot. The first was the impact of isolation. Over time I discovered that it helped me not feel so alone when I learned that other leaders deal with the same issue. This awareness didn't necessarily solve my problems, but it did help me realize I wasn't the only leader working through this. Isolation can be a harsh taskmaster. We just weren't meant to lead this way.

The second was understanding where the battle is being fought. In reality, the most intense battles take place in our minds. It's unlikely that anyone in your life really knows what you are thinking continuously. Even the most talkative leader can carry on conversations that are more fluff than fact. The battlefield of the mind is where the greatest conflicts occur. I'm sure even Moses could relate to us.

Do you ever wonder what Moses thought about while tending his father-in-law's flock? Maybe he had once believed he was born for a great purpose. I wonder whether his family told him the story of how he was saved as a baby. No matter what he thought of himself, a failed attempt to help out a brother caused everything in his life to fall apart when he murdered the Egyptian (Ex. 2:1–15). This failure took him into a desert to tend sheep for forty years.

Moses had a lot of time to replay his failure over and over and over again. After all, there wasn't much else to do in the desert. It would have been easy to develop thought patterns of negative beliefs about himself with so much time on his hands. This is why he immediately tried to tell God that he couldn't become the leader that God said he already was (3:7–11). He was willing to give up on his calling because of a disempowering view of himself.

When we read the burning bush story in Exodus 3:1–5, most folks focus on the burning bush and God speaking to Moses from it. However, there is a valuable lesson in this encounter for leaders who thought they would be there by now. The lesson comes from God commanding Moses, "Remove your sandals from your feet. You're standing on holy ground" (v. 5).

Why did God tell him to take off his sandals? I first heard this explained by Pastor Jack Hayford at the Promise Keepers pastors' conference in Atlanta years ago. He taught three reasons Moses needed to take off his shoes when he was on holy ground:

1. He would have stepped in sheep dung at some point in the past.
2. He most likely made his sandals himself. (Payless Sandals didn't have an outlet in the desert.)
3. The sand was hot under his feet, so he had to keep shifting them.

How does this relate to you and me?

First, you can't step into your created purpose as long as you have the poop of the past stuck to you. At some point you're going to have to stop thinking about the past. Next, you can't fulfill your purpose using your own talents and resources. You must depend on His ability to work *through* you. Then, you will need to stay in step with the Holy Spirit and keep moving in the direction He leads you.

Perhaps it's time to take off your shoes. Are you ready to get in step with the Holy Spirit and start moving in the direction He leads you? Take a moment right now and begin picturing yourself as a conduit of God's glory on the earth. I promise that He still wants to use you as a kingdom expander.

THE TWEET THAT CHANGED MY LIFE

During the time when I was living under constant pressure, I often contemplated packing up and heading out to Montana, otherwise known as Big Sky Country. I imagined that living off the land would somehow relieve the weight of failure that seemed to crush me at every turn. Yet I knew that running wasn't the answer.

At the pinnacle of the struggle between my feelings of failure and my desire to embrace freedom, my friend Shane Duffey posted a simple message on Twitter that forever altered one of my false beliefs:

"You can't let God down because you're not holding Him up."

Boom! The timing of Shane's post was perfect. I felt like I had just been punched in the stomach—in a good way. In that moment I felt something change on the inside.

Shane's tweet isn't exactly breaking news. But for me, it was spot on. God used this simple statement to break through decades of wrong thinking that had shaped who I had become. In that moment I released it all. Everything I had been holding in for years came flooding out. I had to pull over on the side of the road and weep because I was too emotional to drive.

Jesus unraveled years of believing that certain people's eternal destiny depended on me. He showed me that I could not save people. My calling is to obediently walk with Him on a daily basis and follow His promptings and guidance. While He certainly wants to work *through* me, I no longer believed He needed me to do things *for* Him.

From that day forward, my daily prayer has been different. I no longer ask Jesus to delay His return until I can get it together. Now my simple prayer is "Jesus, live through me today however You want." My biggest desire is to be a conduit of His blessing as I stay connected to Him every day.

The euphoria of having Jesus heal my spiritual heart was somewhat dampened when I found out the need for healing of my physical heart. I had lived so many years under the stress of failed performance that it had affected my health. Thankfully, the peace I was now living in provided so much comfort as I went through quadruple bypass surgery.

YOU CAN'T LET GOD DOWN BECAUSE YOU'RE NOT

HOLDING HIM UP.

Pastor, isn't it time to stop measuring yourself against the church down the street? Would you be willing to join me today and put down the weight you've been carrying? Can you let go of denominational expectations? Or the expectations of your church leaders? Or, especially, the wrong beliefs you have developed about success? A leader who is connected to the Source has nothing to prove to anyone. That leader has accepted the role of being a pipeline of blessing. Just not the source of blessing.

Today I am a pipeline of blessing. I'm a vessel. A simple pipe that He can flow through as He chooses. The pressure to perform is gone. The dread of seeing disappointment on His face when I finally see Him for the first time is gone. The intimidation I felt when bumping into a more successful leader is gone. It's all gone.

In the place of all those feelings is peace, purpose, and fulfillment. I now truly believe He will finish what He started in me. I'm not worried about being a failure anymore. My greatest responsibility is to stay connected to Him. I am successful because I am in Him and He is in me. He is my life.

Jesus gave me a gift through Shane that changed the trajectory of my life as well as ministry. He wants to do the same for you. Don't wait as long as I did to embrace the benefit of living in freedom. No matter what you do or do not accomplish, "you can't let God down because you're not holding Him up." When you let go of the wrong belief that you are somehow responsible for the results of people's choices, you will be free to be a vessel of His joy and fulfillment. You will find that more people are drawn to you and your ministry because of what they see in you.

WHO'S IN CHARGE?

Several years ago, a friend explained to me the challenges of owning a stallion. I don't have any experience with horses, so I was fascinated by his insight. He said a stallion has to be reminded who is in charge every single day. The horse will give the owner fits if it senses a lack of resolve.

He said you can ride a stallion or spend an entire day cooperating on various tasks. However, as you greet the stallion the next morning, it will look you in the eye as if to ask, *Who's in charge today?* This was so enlightening. Apparently, a stallion's challenge of *Who's in charge?* will continue throughout its life.

This example relates perfectly to what I have to deal with every day. You will discover the same is true for you. The difficulty you will face going forward is that your issues won't simply go away because you decided to get healthy. I still deal with measuring my success in relation to my performance. Just like the owner of the stallion, I am consistently challenged with "Who's in charge today?" Performance or grace? By God's grace, I refuse to revert to my old, disempowering way of thinking. Although the question never ceases, meeting it consistently is the only way to ensure I don't give up.

If you think about it, you can't have a victory unless you fight the battle. But there isn't a magic bullet to getting past thinking you would be there by now. You didn't get here quickly, and your thought patterns won't change overnight. However, I can promise that you can change. It starts with a decision and becomes reality as you carry out your convictions. You will find that living in victory becomes easier as you change your thought patterns and develop right habits. Knowing *where* the battle is being fought also helps you be more strategic in pursuing lasting victory.

You cannot win the conflict of "Who's in charge?" if you engage from a position of misinformation. Here are three challenges you are likely to encounter as you begin to change.

CHALLENGE 1: ASSESS YOUR GIFTEDNESS HONESTLY

Is it true that you can be anything you want to be? Truthfully, no, you can't. While it is a popular slogan to say to our children, I think it is one of the biggest reasons so many of us feel like failures in the church world. How many times have you endured a tone-deaf soloist who was encouraged to "share his or her gift" with the world? You can only be your best when you are using your spiritual gifts and natural talents. Just because you want to do something doesn't necessarily mean you are gifted to do it.

This is why it is so important to be honest when assessing the results you've produced so far. It's one thing to need training, experience, and opportunities to grow. It's another thing entirely to continue pursuing a path you clearly aren't gifted for. Nothing will cause you to think you should be there by now faster than trying to do something you are not equipped to do.

CHALLENGE 2: EVALUATE YOUR LEADERSHIP PRIORITIES

To be an effective leader, you must prioritize your leadership responsibilities in the proper sequence. Remember that your focus can't be only on having success today. True success continues beyond the present and eventually builds a lasting legacy. Many leaders have appeared to be successful because of the size of the organizations they have built. However, their success proved to be unsustainable because their leadership priorities were not in proper sequence. You must have the proper priorities in place when facing the "Who's in charge?" challenge.

THE SEQUENCE FOR LEADERSHIP SUCCESS

1. Leading yourself. Your first responsibility is to develop the personal disciplines needed to maintain a healthy, balanced life. It's up to you to maintain a vibrant and growing walk with Jesus. It's up to you to take care of your physical body through exercise, proper eating, and rest. You are responsible for the stewardship of your finances. People who lead themselves well are capable of leading others well.

2. Leading your spouse. Great marriages don't happen by chance. It takes intentionality to keep your marriage strong. I made the commitment to Gina many years ago that I would never choose ministry over our marriage. So

I resolved that I would leave the ministry to save my marriage if necessary. For me, it's nonnegotiable. Ministry will never become "the other woman" in my heart.

It's okay to get help if you're having marriage problems. I met with a pastor several years ago who lost his church while in the midst of losing his marriage. When I asked him how this situation happened, he responded, "To be honest, our marriage has been in trouble for several years." I replied, "Then why in the world didn't you get help?" I was stunned at how nonchalantly he spoke. He seemed to think I would assume that having a bad marriage is one of the sacrifices of serving in ministry. I want every pastor and other leader to know that this isn't true. You can lead a ministry and have a great marriage too. But only if you're intentional.

3. Leading your children. Few vocations have yielded more brokenness between parents and their children than serving in ministry. This is such a sad statement. However, many leaders accept that being an absentee parent goes with the territory, much as my friend assumed about his failing marriage. Friends, this belief has to change.

Next to leading yourself and your spouse, you have no greater leadership responsibility than leading your children. You are the greatest influencer your children know. Your ability to shape their image of who God is and how He interacts with us can't be understated. Far too many PKs (preachers' kids) have grown up watching their parents serve everyone else at the expense of their own families. In many instances, our children leave home with a disdain for Jesus, church, and the ministry because of our failure to prioritize them.

4. Leading your team. We are in such an exciting season in the church because many of us are discovering the importance of leading through teams. I believe Jesus is drawing us back to the instructions Paul recorded in Ephesians 4. Our first priority as spiritual leaders is to equip saints to do ministry (vv. 11–12). And no one but Jesus should be the main focus.

Whether you lead a paid staff, volunteers, or some combination of both, the priority of leading and developing your team is paramount. A surprising number of staff and volunteers feel frustrated when it comes to serving under their leaders. Because of the lack of clarity about expectations, many of them feel as though they were thrown into the deep end when they agreed to serve.

When it's all said and done, it's important to know that you perpetuate what you tolerate. But a well-thought-out plan accompanied by consistent follow-through will enable you to win the "Who's in charge?" battle.

YOU PERPETUATE WHAT YOU TOLERATE.

CHALLENGE 3: EMBRACE THE ROLE OF EQUIPPER

News flash: the call in Ephesians 4 to become an equipper isn't optional. Equipping others is the only way to achieve effective and lasting impact. While this is true in all fields, it especially applies to the local church. For decades the priority of developing leaders has been completely ignored in most Christian circles. I think this is why 95 percent of American churches remain small. They can only grow to the level of their leaders.

All leaders, no matter the size of their organizations, face what I call challenge barriers, much like the stallion that my friend greets every morning. Each new level of leadership success brings challenges to be confronted. The practices that got you to your current level are not sufficient to overcome the new challenges of leading at a higher level.

Any crack in your leadership resolve will cause you to stay at your current level. There is always another mountain to climb. Unfortunately, this reality goes with the territory of leading.

This truth has a tremendous effect on churches of all sizes. Leaders of small churches often hold to the misconception that leaders of larger ministries don't face the same challenges to their personal leadership. This is not the case at all. Every leader faces the "Who's in charge?" challenge, even those who have experienced a measure of success. The only difference between us and them is that they have conquered a few more challenges.

Remember, past victories do not automatically guarantee future success. You must prepare, evaluate, and purpose to meet each new challenge with the same ferocity as you conquered the last. Inability—or unwillingness—to meet the challenge will always result in stopped momentum.

EQUIPPING OTHERS IS THE ONLY WAY TO ACHIEVE

EFFECTIVE AND LASTING IMPACT.

It is true that training a stallion is hard work. However, anyone who has ridden a stallion will tell you there is nothing like it. The reward is more than worth the effort because it allows you to experience life at a level few will ever understand.

Each new leadership level you encounter requires you to confront the challenges with resolve and commitment. You will probably find, as I have, that the greatest challenge of all is answering "Who's in charge?" Determine now that you will never grow weary in confronting this question. You have the Holy Spirit of God living inside you. Allow Him to infuse you with the courage to face your internal challenger and embrace the possibilities in front of you.

DIGGING DEEPER

1. What issues have caused you to withdraw into isolation? List the measures you will put in place to overcome this tendency.
2. Understanding that the battlefield is in your mind, name five things you can do to keep renewing it with consistency. Whom will you share these things with? By when?
3. How do you react when you face the question "Who's in charge?" Describe what you do well and what you need to address in your leadership when challenged.
4. Does your current role match up with your gifts? Take some time to compare what you're good at and what you enjoy with what is asked of you in your current position. Would you attend your church or participate in your ministry if you were not being paid to serve there? List what you like and don't like about it.
5. Are you leading your home well? Write down how you think your spouse and each of your children would answer this question.

9

THE SWEET SPOT

If your actions create a legacy that inspires others to dream more, learn more, do more and become more, then, you are an excellent leader.

—Dolly Parton

Removing the weight of unmet expectations can be both freeing and confusing at the same time. Having that burden lifted will bring tremendous peace. You may also experience a new kind of tension as you begin to wonder what the next steps are.

Many well-meaning leaders will advise you to take a leap of faith when facing a new opportunity or challenge. However, taking a leap of faith is neither biblical nor wise. The majority of us who follow the leaping advice end up experiencing the crash of reality. Growing deeper in your spiritual walk is more like taking steps of faith rather than leaps. Steps of faith allow you to see where to go next methodically. A blind leap will usually land you in a mess.

I'm sure David in the Bible had many occasions to walk in the dark of night as he tended sheep. No doubt he used a lantern to light his way as he traversed the rugged plains. The lantern would illuminate all the area around him, unlike the direct beam of a flashlight. Although he couldn't see far, he could see enough to navigate each step. Without a lantern's wide glow, it would be possible to miss the dangers lurking close by.

Letting go of thinking you would be there by now and embracing your calling with passion and purpose is a remarkable experience. But now is not the time to take a blind leap into the unknown. On the contrary, now is the time to make solid choices based on whom God created you to be and the gifts He placed in you at birth. As David learned while tending sheep, "Your word is a lamp to my feet and a light to my path" (Ps. 119:105 NKJV). As you plan for the future, allow God's Word to guide you and help you grow in faith.

Growing in faith also requires an intentional building process. Count the costs of what you are building. Make sure you have a firm foundation. Don't cut corners on the construction. And intentionally allow Jesus to decorate the project as He always intended.

This chapter will provide clarity for making the right choices to help you be all that He created you to be as you lead *from* Him. I'm so excited for you to move into the wonderful season of ministry joy that awaits you. I know your fruitfulness will overflow in this next season. The next generation will walk in their purpose because you walk in yours.

THE UNKNOWN SWEET SPOT

Have you ever heard Jesus speak directly to you through someone else? Sometimes His message is something you have been searching for. Other times He unexpectedly reveals what's coming next in your life. In either case, you know on the inside that He is calling you out.

I was on a staff planning retreat a few years ago when the latter happened to me. It was at a time when I was finally content with the trajectory my life was on. Although I never would have declared that I had arrived, I was confident that Jesus was going to use me as executive pastor of my church and as a consultant for the Unstuck Group for the foreseeable future. It was such a fulfilling season.

Imagine, then, the discomfort I started feeling when I realized that Jesus had something to say to me concerning my future. During the retreat, I asked my friend Brad Cooper to lead a devotion for our team. As Brad was walking to the front of the room, he shared that he had been impressed by the Holy Spirit to change his original message. Clearly something was about to happen. I learned a long time ago to be especially receptive when speakers say the Lord changed their message on the day of an event.

Brad began his talk by drawing a large circle on the whiteboard. Inside the circle he wrote phrases that describe a successful ministry. He referred to the circle as our sweet spot of ministry. He continued by discussing how Jesus will lead us into the sweet spot, where we will experience fruitfulness and contentment. This comes from knowing we are exactly where He wants us to be and doing exactly what He created us to do. So far I was tracking right along with Brad. After all, I had finally let go of thinking I would be there by now and had joyfully accepted that I was right where God wanted me.

Soon, however, Brad changed things up on us. While continuing to talk about ministering in our sweet spot, he drew another circle in the upper right corner of the whiteboard. He labeled it "The Unknown Sweet Spot." Then he shared how the Lord had been showing him earlier that morning that He often has another sweet spot for us, which we will never experience until we are faithful and contented in our current sweet spot.

In other words, contented faithfulness where you are today will often open opportunities you didn't even consider possible.

I knew in that moment that Jesus was about to take me to a new place in ministry. And for the first time in my life, I wasn't sure I wanted to go anywhere new. I was experiencing unprecedented success at what I was doing—finally. Did I really want to give this up to take on another opportunity? In all honesty, I really didn't want to change.

THE UNKNOWN SWEET SPOT

THE UNKNOWN SWEET SPOT
PURPOSE   INFLUENCE
GREATER IMPACT   OPPORTUNITY
SUPERNATURAL PROVISION

THE SWEET SPOT

SUCCESS	CONNECTION
DISCIPLESHIP	COMMUNITY
SALVATION	BLESSING
FULLFILLMENT	PEACE
JOY	FRUIT

During Brad's talk, I sensed Jesus impressing on me that He had something else for me to do. I would have to let go of my current comfort and its accompanying sense of security in order to step into another area of ministry. Although I really loved the people I was serving alongside at the local church, I knew it was only a matter of time before I said yes to this next season of life.

After a few months of personal turmoil, I accepted the position of executive director of 95Network. There was no way to know in that moment exactly what God had in store for my life. I often say I went kicking and screaming into blessing. It was painful to let go of what I was holding on to at the time. I wanted to hold on to the security I had. I also didn't want to step down from the team at Unstuck. However, I never could have dreamed of the opportunities that have opened up since I said yes to His direction.

THE SWEET SPOT OF PURPOSE

Hearing Brad talk about purpose that morning didn't surprise me at all. He has a deep desire to help people understand how to connect their giftings and passion to fulfill their God-given purpose. In fact, he has another illustration he often uses to communicate with people who are searching for God's will in their lives.

It is not an exaggeration to say that Brad has shared this illustration with hundreds of people over the years. In fact, the majority of people he has met with over the past decade can testify about him drawing the Sweet Spot diagram on a napkin in a coffee shop or restaurant. His insight into how to know the will of God and His purpose for your life is thoroughly practical.

This insight applies to you too. We all need guidance at times. Whom should I connect with? What do I need to do differently? When do I start? Where do I go? Why change at all?

After drawing three circles, Brad defined each of them. One represents God's glory, the second represents your joy, and the final circle represents the world's good.

THE SWEET SPOT

God's Glory. The Scriptures make it abundantly clear that our first goal in life is to glorify God, even in our common daily actions: "Whether you eat or drink, or whatever you do, do all to the glory of God" (1 Cor. 10:31 NKJV). The first circle represents God's glory because we should desire to bring glory to God in every aspect of our lives.

Your Joy. The second circle represents the things that bring you joy in this life. Even though many Christians haven't figured this out yet, we were created to live in joy. "Rejoice in the Lord always. I will say it again: Rejoice!" (Phil. 4:4 NIV). Also, according to Nehemiah, "The joy of the LORD is your strength" (8:10 NIV). We are expected to live lives of joy as believers.

However, we should keep in mind two critically important truths concerning joy.

WHILE HAPPINESS IS OFTEN DETERMINED BY WHAT'S HAPPENING AROUND YOU, JOY FLOWS FROM WHAT IS HAPPENING INSIDE YOU.

First, the joy of the Lord and happiness are not the same. While happiness is often determined by what's happening around you, joy flows from what is happening inside you. Christians deal with the same sufferings and setbacks as everyone else. But as Christians, the highs and lows of life should not defeat us.

We can begin living in the joy of the Lord when we accept the fact that we're not in control. Joy is available when we let go of worrying about everything and begin to rest in His perfect plan for our lives. I still don't like the patience required to live this way, but it's impossible to experience His assuring presence any other way.

Second, your joy will never be in opposition to God's Word. There are obviously some things in this life that will bring temporary joy yet are in direct opposition to Scripture. It is never wise to trump God's Word with what you want simply because it brings you joy.

The World's Good. The final circle represents God's intention in creating each one of us. His master plan is for us to be involved in advancing His kingdom throughout the world. I believe this is especially critical when it comes to reaching the next generation. Ephesians 2:10 says, "We are His workmanship" (NKJV). Every one of us has the purpose of bringing the hope of the gospel to others. There is no higher calling or purpose in life than helping people find Jesus.

The church is called to preach the gospel and expand the kingdom of God. It's up to us because Jesus provided no plan B. You and I are commissioned to bring light into the darkness. We are also here to ensure the next generation is firmly planted on solid ground as we hand off the ministry to them. We are here for the world's good in order that they may know Him.

WE ARE HERE FOR THE WORLD'S GOOD IN ORDER THAT

THEY MAY KNOW HIM.

Brad's diagram clearly shows how to determine your God-given sweet spot. It happens where God's glory, your joy, and the world's good intersect. Understanding your purpose in each of these areas is critical to finding your sweet spot. It is imperative that you be willing to make all necessary adjustments in the way you are currently operating in order to get there.

A time may come in which you find yourself in the same place I was. You are finally content in your sweet spot, and suddenly opportunity comes knocking. Jesus begins to whisper to you about your unknown sweet spot. Like me, you might resist the first nudges. If you do, please remember this: *your sweet spot can become a sour spot if you stay there too long.*

One of the biggest challenges you and I will face in leadership is not being able to recognize when the current season is over and it's time for a change. It is possible for a wonderful season of fruitful ministry to turn sour when your time has come to an end but you resist acknowledging it.

Here are eight indicators that you are on the verge of allowing your sweet spot to turn sour:

1. You can no longer motivate those you lead to take action.
2. You no longer enjoy the day-to-day tasks required by the job.
3. Your trust in those around you is severely diminishing.
4. You seldom see new converts in your ministry.
5. Your attitude about sermon prep shifts from anticipation to going through the motions.
6. You invest the majority of your energy in activities away from ministry.
7. You have no desire to invest resources to reach the next generation.
8. You would not attend your church if you weren't getting paid.

Thousands of pastors and other leaders in our churches today feel stalled in this way. If they were honest, they would admit they no longer desire to see their ministries succeed. However, tenure has caused them to become dependent on the income from the job. If they refuse to step out when the time is right, they will become passionless leaders of passionless ministries. Sometimes our desire for security limits our willingness to follow the Lord's leading to the next adventure, especially as we get older. Eventually we wake up to find that the missed opportunity has limited our purpose and effectiveness in the long haul.

I don't believe we ever fully retire from ministry. Obviously, responsibilities change with age, but the calling to ministry is a lifelong call. This is why it's critical to understand your sweet spot and recognize how it changes over the years.

I am really looking forward to seeing Jesus face to face. I hope He will give me a little fist pump and say, "Thank you, Dale, for helping My church." I most likely will end up on my face, worshipping Him and thanking Him for saving me and calling me into His service. I hope you have this anticipation too. If not, then it's time to find your sweet spot of purpose. Maybe some things are different for you now. But don't spend another day thinking you should be there by now. Move forward today by walking in what brings glory to God, joy to you, and good to the world.

DIGGING DEEPER

1. Reflect on a time or two when you took a leap of faith that didn't turn out so well. What lessons did you learn from each experience?
2. How would you describe your ministry sweet spot? What are its attributes?
3. To help you clarify your sweet spot, answer this question from chapter 7: "What would you do if you knew you couldn't fail?" Be bold as you write out the dream that's in your heart. Next, list the barriers that are keeping you from pursuing it.
4. What process do you use to determine when it's time to embrace change? How would you advise someone who asked you how to know when it's time for a change?

10

THE HANDOFF

The end of an era is not the completion of a destiny.
Just because something's over, don't stop!

—Brian Houston

When I started out, I thought I knew the main purpose of writing this book. My desire was to bring encouragement and renewal to the many pastors and other leaders who have become disillusioned in their dream of being used by Jesus to make a difference. I felt that sharing my story would cause others to realize that ministry was never meant to be about our performance. I decided that painfully reliving some of the valleys of my journey was worth it if somehow it could help other leaders avoid the same pitfalls.

I was pleasantly surprised, however, as the Lord later helped me see His greater purpose for this book and, in some ways, my life experiences. I have become increasingly aware that my journey is quite similar to many other leaders'. The Holy Spirit helped me see a carefully constructed plan to destroy the effectiveness of pastors all around the world. This plan isn't just to defeat the church of today. It's much more than that.

At its core, the plan is to destroy the ability of the church today to have a lasting impact on the church of tomorrow. It's not enough for Satan to discourage you and defeat your ministry. He wants to distract you from one of the greatest responsibilities you have—creating a vibrant ministry that you hand off to the next generation. His plan is really this simple. If Satan can get you to give up on the church of today, then he can be sure you will give up on the church of tomorrow. Recognizing the sad reality that thousands of churches are closing each year, we must come together now to stand against this negative trend.

I'm not being overly dramatic when I say that the future of the church and the eternal destiny of millions hang in the balance. We simply cannot afford to fail when it comes to handing off healthy churches to the next generation.

WE SIMPLY CANNOT AFFORD TO FAIL WHEN IT COMES TO HANDING OFF HEALTHY CHURCHES TO THE NEXT GENERATION.

The Bible says, "We also, since we are surrounded by so great a cloud of witnesses, let us lay aside every weight, and the sin which so easily ensnares us, and let us run with endurance the race that is set before us, looking unto Jesus, the author and finisher of our faith, who for the joy that was set before Him endured the cross, despising the shame, and has sat down at the right hand of the throne of God" (Heb. 12:1–2 NKJV).

You have probably taught on this passage many times. As I was growing up, many communicators made sure I understood what kind of race the Hebrew writer was referring to. They would explain that the race we are in as Christians is not a sprint but a marathon. They used this metaphor to teach that we should prepare to serve Jesus for the long haul instead of running wide open and quickly running out of energy.

While it is great advice to carefully plot your life's course, a little more study of the context of this passage reveals that the race we are in is neither a sprint nor a marathon. It's much more.

In the previous chapter, we read, "All these, having obtained a good testimony through faith, did not receive the promise, God having provided something better for us, that they should not be made perfect apart from us" (Heb. 11:39–40 NKJV).

The phrase "made perfect" in the original language is a form of the word *teleioō*, which means "to complete, accomplish, carry through to the end, bring to a successful conclusion, reach a goal, fulfill."[15] I used to be confused by verse 40—"God having provided something better for us"—because the context of chapter 11 is about the heroes of the faith. However, "made perfect" makes sense when you look back at verse 39: "All these, having obtained a good testimony through faith, did not receive the promise." Those who have gone before us could not complete something apart from us. What could they not complete? The race. They were unable to complete the race because it's actually a relay race.

Those verses in Hebrews connect the lives of those who have gone before us with our lives today through the metaphor of a relay race. This is why it says that they can't be made perfect, or complete, apart from us. Through this relay race, you and I are connected to Moses, Elijah, and all the saints who have gone before us. This is why Hebrews 12:1 says, "We are surrounded by so great a cloud of witnesses" (NKJV).

Once the saints who have gone before us complete their laps, they take their places in the stands until everyone who will follow them has completed the race too. What does this mean for us today? It means that Moses, Elijah, the prophets, and everyone else needs us to complete our laps in order for them to finish the race. The stadium is packed with runners who have completed their laps and are now cheering us on.

Consider that your discouragement really may come from the Enemy attempting to get you to botch the exchange. Remember that a relay isn't just about speed. Certainly, speed is important. However, it's just as important to successfully hand off the baton to the next runner.

Missing the exchange will result in lost momentum. Even more sobering is the understanding that you will lose the race if you fail to hand off the baton to the next runner. You might wonder what can be done about that. Eugene Peterson's paraphrase of Hebrews 12:1 states that we need to "strip down, start running—and never quit! No extra spiritual fat, no parasitic sins." The NIV tells us, "Let us throw off everything that hinders and the sin that so easily entangles."

We're all aware of sins that interrupt our race. But most of us may not have given enough attention to the weights we've been carrying. Look at how the NKJV states it: "Let us lay aside every *weight*, and the sin which so easily ensnares us, and let us run with endurance the race that is set before us" (emphasis added). It is imperative that we set aside every weight. We can do this by addressing four weights that can cause us to miss the exchange: depression, deception, dehydration, and distraction.

DEPRESSION

I believe depression begins as oppression. The Enemy opposes us as we set out to run our race. This opposition certainly creates drag that can slow us down. But it doesn't stop us entirely. Only after a season of unrelenting oppression does the oppression morph into depression.

Thankfully, we can overcome an oppressive attack before it becomes depression by reminding ourselves that Jesus provided armor for us (Eph. 6:11–17). And Paul revealed that we cannot fight spiritual battles with carnal weapons (2 Cor. 10:4). It is imperative that you and I stand against the oppression that Satan brings against us if we are going to run the race effectively.

If oppression morphs into depression, it can be a heavy weight that hinders or stops you. Depression is a serious matter. I am not qualified to speak about this issue from a clinical or medical perspective. Qualified professional guidance is imperative if you are suffering from extreme depression or any form of mental illness. Don't be embarrassed to seek help. The goal is for you to be whole and free to fulfill your calling.

DECEPTION

As you know, deception leads to sin, and the effects of sin will stop us in our tracks. The best way to avoid deception is to meditate on God's Word, spend time in prayer, and submit to accountability.

However, if you are entrapped in habitual sin, you've already been deceived. It may take awhile, but you can be assured your sins will find you out (Num. 32:23), and the consequences may be devastating.

God's Word is never wrong. Galatians teaches that we always reap what we sow (6:7–9). If you have given in to sin, I'm sure you didn't intend to end up where you are today. The process happened slowly. Just a little here and there. You were deceived into playing with temptation. But soon you found yourself being controlled by something other than your heart for God. Deception gains a stronghold if you tell yourself it doesn't have any power over you.

ANY SIN CAN BE FORGIVEN, AND RESTORATION CAN BE

EXPERIENCED BY THE TRULY CONTRITE AND HUMBLE

LEADER.

The obvious solution is to repent—today. Any sin can be forgiven, and restoration can be experienced by the truly contrite and humble leader. First you must break the bonds of deception and tell yourself the truth. Then admit the truth to your spouse or another leader. Don't put it off another day. You will definitely need to take a break from ministry until you confront your issues and develop solid habits. However, your willingness to repent, seek accountability, and commit to restoration will bless so many people in the future. You'll be able to joyfully run your race, unencumbered.

DEHYDRATION

We are admonished to run with endurance. The definition of *endurance* is "patience, steadfastness, or constancy." According to Thayer's Greek Lexicon, *endurance* in the New Testament is "the characteristic of a man who is unswerved from his deliberate purpose and his loyalty to faith and piety by even the greatest trials and sufferings."[16] In order to endure a long race, a runner must avoid the exhaustion that comes with dehydration.

As I mentioned earlier, I have struggled with patience throughout my life. As I have grown older, my times of discouragement usually come when I'm faced with a situation that requires patient endurance. Long seasons of waiting for answers or breakthroughs eventually lead to exhaustion. But when you think about it, isn't that the point? The Enemy knows that exhausted leaders most likely will want to give up on running their laps in this relay race. Exhaustion causes us to give out and give up.

The only way for runners to avoid exhaustion is to make sure they are nourished and hydrated. Dehydration is certain if they fail to drink enough water to continue the race.

EXHAUSTION CAUSES US TO GIVE OUT AND GIVE UP.

We can easily become spiritually dehydrated due to a lack of intentional replenishment. In his book *Replenish: Leading from a Healthy Soul*, Lance Witt wrote, "You can no more wish spiritual health into existence than you can wish physical health into existence."[17] Wishing health into your life never works. Neglecting the disciplines required to maintain spiritual health always leads to exhaustion.

I've adopted five margin makers that have helped me stay spiritually, relationally, and physically hydrated. You may find them useful as well. Feel free to customize them to fit your life.

MARGIN MAKER 1: SCHEDULE PERSONAL SOUL CARE INTO YOUR CALENDAR

You and I have to be intentional about making time on a daily basis for exercise, reflection, and replenishment. This will happen only if you block out time on your daily calendar for yourself. By the way, you have to honor it too. Far too many of us sacrifice our own personal well-being in order to help others. If you continue to run this way, you'll find yourself out of the race. But if you make soul care a nonnegotiable appointment, you'll improve your relay stats significantly.

MARGIN MAKER 2: CREATE A WEEKLY DATE NIGHT WITH YOUR SPOUSE

If you're married, the fastest way to lose your marriage is to take for granted that your spouse understands the pressures of ministry. Stresses and interruptions obviously come along with the responsibilities of pastoring. However, they are never a valid excuse for neglecting your marriage.

Proverbs 5 details how people allow themselves to be involved in adultery. Verse 18 states, "May you rejoice in the wife of your youth" (NIV). Malachi 2:14–15 also confronts the person who is unfaithful to the wife of his youth. Do not allow your ministry to become your mistress.

As a leader, it is imperative that you maintain the joyful relationship you had when you first were married. Jesus does not want you to lose your marriage in order to serve His church. And by the way, marriage care is another form of soul care. Enjoy time with your spouse, and watch the effects it has on your ministry.

MARGIN MAKER 3: HONOR THE SABBATH PRINCIPLE EACH WEEK

I have often said that God modeled the Sabbath principle for us in the creation story and He wasn't even tired. The Sabbath principle means you take a literal day off each week and do something you enjoy that is not necessarily ministry related.

One of the purposes of Sabbath is to reconnect you with your heavenly Father. I believe He gave us the principles of Sabbath and tithing in order to remind us that He is our source. Neglect Sabbath, and you will soon find yourself believing that you are your source. Adopt a Sabbath habit, and watch God provide everything you need, including time.

MARGIN MAKER 4: BECOME AN EQUIPPER OF YOUR FLOCK

I don't think it's possible to fully embrace your calling as a pastor without equipping your people to do ministry. We've already noted that equipping is a must in order for a ministry to become sustainable and self-perpetuating (Eph. 4:11–16). Pastor, if you want to discover the rhythm required for long-term ministry, you must allow others to share your load. Simply put, your church will have a much greater and lasting impact when you pass the baton to other leaders.

MARGIN MAKER 5: PLAN A YEARLY EXTENDED VACATION WITH YOUR FAMILY

We all need something to look forward to in the midst of our weekly routine. Planning an annual vacation gives you encouragement, because you know that a break from the stresses of day-to-day ministry will soon be here. It also communicates to your family that they are a top priority to you. Neglecting an annual vacation communicates to them that your ministry is more important to you than they are. Taking extended time off will often help your family reconnect and maintain the bond that makes your home special.

When we try to function in ministry without creating margin for healthy soul care, we will eventually become self-deceived. The biggest problem with self-deception is that we get used to it. Lance also stated in *Replenish*,

> The greatest danger, really, isn't in projecting a false image; there's a Pharisee inside all of us, and I suspect we'll struggle with this as long as we live. The greatest danger is in getting comfortable with it, learning how to "succeed" with a disconnected soul. Over time we can become very adept at playing the image-management game. The truth is you don't have to have a healthy soul to be seen as a success in ministry.[18]

As heartbreaking as the comment is, I have to agree with Lance when he said, "You don't have to have a healthy soul to be seen as a success in ministry." However, an unhealthy leader is at great risk of being disqualified from the race. Remember, you can no more wish yourself into endurance than you can wish away a physical sickness.

Only through intentional margin will you find the endurance needed to hand off the baton.

DISTRACTION

Finally, to ensure we complete our laps and hand off the baton, we must keep our eyes on the prize. We have acknowledged that we must not allow ourselves to become depressed as a result of unchallenged oppression. We confronted the deception that stops us in our tracks when sin is allowed to go unaddressed in our lives. And we listed some proven margin makers to help us avoid dehydration and endure until it's time to pass the baton.

The writer of Hebrews instructs us to "lay aside every weight, and the sin which so easily ensnares us" and encourages us to "run with endurance" (12:1 NKJV). The second verse exhorts us to look to Jesus, which guarantees our success. We can avoid depression, deception, and dehydration by fixing our gaze on Jesus as our sustaining source.

Remember that a regular guy like Peter was able to walk on water as long as he kept his eyes on Jesus. He began to sink only after he allowed himself to become distracted by the wind and waves around him (Matt. 14:28–30). He turned his focus to his surroundings.

If you and I are going to avoid distraction, we should learn to follow Jesus' example. He focused on the joy set before Him in order to endure the cross (Heb. 12:2). As you run your lap and prepare to hand off the baton, what is the joy set before you?

Here are some ideas that bring me incredible joy as I run my lap:

- knowing I'll see Jesus face to face—I plan to thank Him for all eternity
- seeing small and midsize churches grow in health and numbers

- seeing the next generation encouraged and empowered by us
- seeing my family and friends fulfill their purpose while enjoying life
- becoming less and seeing Jesus become more in the years I have left
- seeing the greatest revival ever cover America with His grace
- seeing the gospel spread around the world until every soul has heard it

These things motivate me. The joy set before me is to run my lap, hand off the baton, and take my place in the stands with all the others who have run before me.

The peace that came from learning it's not up to me to make anything happen has been the most important breakthrough I have experienced in my ministry and in writing this book. Jesus never wanted me to do it all on my own. And He was gracious enough to allow me the time to figure it out.

What about you, my friend? You now understand that your race is much more than a sprint or marathon. It's really not about you or me at all. I invite you to join me in building a powerful team of track stars who will not only run their laps but also train those coming up behind them to run faithfully as well.

DIGGING DEEPER

1. Who comes to mind as you think about handing off the baton?
2. What are some ways you can be intentional about handing off your ministry? Identify at least five young potential leaders you can disciple.

3. Determine your personal list of margin makers. Write out each one with a detailed description of what it is, whom it impacts, how you will implement it, and when you're going to initiate it.

4. With whom will you share the joy set before you? Create a list of the things that bring you joy.

AFTERWORD

Earlier we looked at how Elijah became so discouraged that he prayed to die: "He came to a lone broom bush and collapsed in its shade, wanting in the worst way to be done with it all—to just die: 'Enough of this, GOD! Take my life—I'm ready to join my ancestors in the grave!' Exhausted, he fell asleep under the lone broom bush" (1 Kings 19:4–5).

I think Elijah experienced the spiritual, physical, and mental trifecta of exhaustion. It was the perfect storm for him. What a terrible place to arrive for anyone, especially someone in the ministry.

It's important to notice, however, that God dealt with Elijah's physical exhaustion *before* addressing his mental and spiritual issues. Pastoring isn't just about being spiritually healthy. Your physical well-being is a must as well.

YOU NEED TO CARE FOR THE TEMPLE GOD HAS GIVEN YOU AND REMEMBER THAT HIS HOLY SPIRIT DWELLS WITHIN YOU.

Many struggling pastors tend to relate to every problem as if it were spiritual. Because of that, they seem to believe that every resolution comes by praying more, reading more, and serving more. While I don't want to negate the importance of prayer, study, and service, you can't ignore the effect your physical well-being has on you. To make it plain, you need to care for the temple God has given you and remember that His Holy Spirit dwells within you (1 Cor. 6:19–20).

Look what happened next with Elijah:

> Suddenly an angel shook him awake and said, "Get up and eat!" He looked around and, to his surprise, right by his head were a loaf of bread baked on some coals and a jug of water. He ate the meal and went back to sleep. The angel of GOD came back, shook him awake again, and said, "Get up and eat some more— you've got a long journey ahead of you." He got up, ate and drank his fill, and set out. Nourished by that meal, he walked forty days and nights, all the way to the mountain of God, to Horeb. (1 Kings 19:5–8)

He slept.

He ate a nourishing meal.

He slept some more.

He ate some more.

He exercised.

It was only after Elijah replenished his physical body that he became ready to discuss his discouragement with God. Taking care of your physical body by resting, eating well, and exercising is a must if you are to arrive *there* and continue beyond *there*.

FREEDOM IS A CONVERSATION AWAY

My journey of healing and transformation began with my confession to a friend that I felt like a failure because I hadn't gotten *there* yet. But the truth is, I was always *there*. Because *there* is wherever Jesus is.

People need to see an authentic, joy-filled church in today's cynical culture. This happens when an authentic, joy-filled pastor is leading it. The time for us to lead by example is now. Our followers need to draw from the security and peace that flow out of our confidence in whose we are and who we are in Him.

My life has changed dramatically in the last few years as I have come to grips with my performance-based lifestyle. Though I never wanted to be one of those people who says, "If I only knew then what I know now," I have become one of them.

My breakthrough came when I verbalized how I felt about myself to my friend Tony. There is something cathartic about unloading your heavy burden out loud. You already know what happens in counseling sessions as you help folks work through their problems. At times it's like the answers everyone is looking for are revealed as they discuss how they arrived where they are. I believe you and I can experience the same breakthroughs as we share our struggles with a trusted friend or counselor.

As pastors and church leaders, we simply can't afford to keep doing what we've always done. My path to healing and wholeness began with an honest confession, and yours can too. However, the journey shouldn't stop there. I have worked through the intricacies of my problems in many conversations over the years. I encourage you to do the same for yourself.

Who can you share your problems with? Here are some suggestions to consider.

FIND A TRUSTED MENTOR

I was able to tell Tony how I felt, because I looked up to him and knew he really cared about me. Think about who you trust, and approach that person honestly.

HIRE A TRAINED COUNSELOR

I'll never forget the first time I heard a well-respected national minister share that he sees a counselor every week. I remember thinking that if he needs a counselor, then I should probably find one as well.

Bob Hamp of Think Differently[19] is a counselor I trust. Although I have never had the privilege of sitting down and talking with him for hours in his office, we have spoken several times over the phone and crossed paths occasionally in person. He lives in the Dallas–Fort Worth area, and I live in South Carolina, but I wouldn't hesitate to go meet with him if I knew I needed to.

TALK TO A FELLOW PASTOR

I have several pastor friends with whom I am comfortable sharing my struggles. The key is to be transparent and feel certain that a fellow pastor loves you unconditionally and believes in God's calling on your life.

Note that you should never bare your soul to someone of the opposite sex unless it's your spouse. Ignoring this absolute is always a recipe for disaster.

TALK TO AN OVERSEER OR ANOTHER LEADER IN YOUR DENOMINATION

Doing so may be hard because you run the risk of having your stability questioned. However, a lot of great overseers have a genuine love for the pastors in their charge. Ask God for direction when considering this option.

SHARE WITH YOUR FAMILY

No one loves me more than my wife and children do. They always want the best for me. They pray for me regularly. Sharing my struggle with them has allowed them to see Jesus do this deep work in my life. It also gives them permission to talk through their issues. If your family relationships are already good, honest conversation at this level can be the passageway to a stronger family bond.

CONNECT WITH 95NETWORK

95Network exists to connect small and midsize churches to big resources. Our vision is to bring positive change to churches everywhere. We would consider it a tremendous privilege to come alongside you. There isn't a week that goes by that I don't have the opportunity to talk with a hurting pastor somewhere. You are the reason we do what we do. You can always get in touch with us through our website, www.95Network.org.

HE FINISHES WHAT HE STARTED

Make a decision today to trust that Jesus knew exactly what He was doing when He called you to be a leader. And remember, He intends for you to walk with Him daily, to trust that He has you exactly where He wants you to be. Are you willing to trust Him today?

We began our journey together by recognizing that we have a major problem unfolding throughout America. Churches from every region and denominational affiliation are closing at alarming rates. Buildings that were once used as houses of worship have been converted into everything from restaurants to nightclubs.

I believe that the small church is the backbone of the church in America. However, the successes and national attention of megachurches have created the false impression that the large church is the norm. Additionally, the notoriety of large-church leaders has inadvertently contributed to the pressure felt by many small-church pastors, causing us to believe we are failures.

Sadly, thousands of churches have drawn a line in the sand when it comes to reaching the next generation. Many have chosen to maintain the status quo over the conscious change required to connect with their surrounding communities. This choice always results in the church ending up on life support. Once on life support, a church has only two options. One, pull the plug and die. Or two, intentionally relaunch with a brand-new mission, vision, and strategy to connect with the community. It's really that cut and dried.

The message of this book can be summed up in two thoughts.

First, understand that *ministry is what you do and not who you are.* It's time to be intentional about letting Jesus use you as a conduit of His love, grace, and power on the earth. The priorities of your life should be God, your family, and then your vocation.

MINISTRY IS WHAT YOU DO AND NOT WHO YOU ARE.

Second, *operate with an urgency to reach the next generation.* This issue has my full attention. We need to understand and accept our responsibility for passing the baton. We must find a way to close the widening generational gap throughout our churches and make it a top priority moving forward.

The future will be bright only if something interrupts the way most churches operate. In his book *The Unstuck Church*, Tony Morgan wrote, "Without the interruption, … the church will remain stuck, and the natural pull will be toward decline and death. Without interruption, death is inevitable. Because of that, I pray God reveals the interruption your church needs to experience its full potential."[20]

Connecting one generation to the next doesn't happen by chance. We must engage in intentional dialogue explaining the strategic plan we will implement. And we should add accountability checkpoints to the plan to ensure we follow through. I am encouraged to see that many churches have chosen to bring in outside help designed to provide clarity and ask the hard questions. Without this help, most churches will dig their heels in deeper in order to maintain the status quo.

Pastor, it is your responsibility to lead your church to connect with the next generation. The importance of this will require a new level of following the Holy Spirit's guidance. I know you can do it. Your best days are still ahead of you.

You thought you would be there by now. So did I. However, I now realize that I actually arrived *there* fifty years ago on a Tuesday night during a spring revival at Mount Airy Baptist Church. That was the time when, as a seven-year-old child, I first heard the Holy Spirit calling me to Himself. That night my mom prayed with me as I asked Jesus into my life. Everything changed for me eternally at that moment.

Sure, there have been highs and lows. I've made enough mistakes and wrong decisions to last a lifetime. However, I made the best decision of my life back then. Obviously, saying yes to Jesus was just the beginning. But now, fifty years later, I understand that He loves me and is as proud of me today as He was back then. I just need to rest in Him and trust what Philippians 1:6 says: "There has never been the slightest doubt in my mind that the God who started this great work in you would keep at it and bring it to a flourishing finish on the very day Christ Jesus appears."

He made you and me each a new creation. If we're willing to trust Him, then we get to see at the end what He had in mind. This journey has helped me realize that He is always thrilled with the results. He is just as thrilled with you. Decide today to let go of your old ways and begin again by enjoying the journey He has for you. After all, He did say, "Apart from me you can do nothing" (John 15:5 NIV).

ACKNOWLEDGMENTS

I want to thank Jesus for being so patient with me. You have allowed me to understand that You made me just the way I am for a reason. It's taken a half century for me to become comfortable with that. Knowing that Your Spirit is with me every step of the way fills me with great hope for the future.

It is not an exaggeration to say I would not be here today without the support and love of my wife, Gina. Thank you, my love, for sticking with me through all the ups and downs of ministry life. You are the most amazing life partner and friend that any man could have ever dreamed of. I love you!

I am so grateful for the encouragement I receive from my family. Tiffany, TJ, Siena, Hannah, Justin, and Lydia are so much more than daughters, sons-in-law, and grandchildren. You are my best friends. I doubt there are many pastors who are prouder of their children than I am. Each of you is a world changer.

My commitment to faithfulness and perseverance is drawn from the example set by my parents, Duree and Gail Sellers, along with my father- and mother-in-law, Ray and Ginny Hyatt. Thank you for modeling for Gina and me how to be relentless in the face of adversity and how to overcome.

Thank you to the team at 95Network—Austin Savage and Stephanie Striegel along with our board of directors and Jim Powell—for your partnership in connecting big resources to small and midsize churches.

Our vision to bring positive change to churches everywhere becomes a little clearer with each new day because of your excellent gifts.

It's so much easier to believe you can accomplish great things when you have a mentor who has pioneered the way. Thank you, Roger Breland, for taking me under your wing. Your willingness to pour into me from your vast wealth of experience shaped so much of who I am today.

Thank you, Tony Morgan, for taking my call on that faithful morning in May. The genuine care you showed allowed me to express how I felt about myself for the first time. Having the opportunity to be a part of the team at the Unstuck Group for a season was one of the highlights of my life. Your passion to help churches get Unstuck inspires me.

I want to thank Kevin Smith, Chris Shaw, Sam and Stephanie Striegel, Nick Hammett, Bernie and Bonnie Iversen, and Jason and Jennifer Guthrie for being some of the greatest encouragers in my life. There is no way to convey how much your friendship has impacted me.

I do not have the ability to express the life-changing impact that Bob Hamp has had on me. Helping me see my need for freedom and discover the problem Jesus came to solve saved my life. I'm forever grateful for you, Bob.

Thank you, Shane Duffey, for the tweet that changed my life. You and Bob hit me with the one-two punch I needed most.

I want to acknowledge Brad, Michael, Clayton, Lee, Alden, and Dan along with Paul, Beth, Howard, and Perry for your friendship and support and for standing with me through some very difficult seasons over the past twenty years.

I am so grateful to Wendi Lord for believing in the message of this book. Your friendship and encouragement helped me to finally be willing to share my story.

It has been such a privilege to be guided through this project by Alice Crider. You are the best! (The exclamation point says it all!)

Thank you to Michael, Judy, Kayla, Jon, Susan, and the team at David C Cook for taking a chance on me. It's such an honor to serve along with you in our effort to help the church experience healthy growth.

NOTES

1. Lisa Cannon Green, "New Churches Draw Those Who Previously Didn't Attend," LifeWay Research, December 8, 2015, https://lifewayresearch.com /2015/12/08/new-churches-draw-those-who-previously-didnt-attend; Jeffrey M. Jones, "U.S. Church Membership Down Sharply in Past Two Decades," Gallup, April 18, 2019, https://news.gallup.com/poll/248837/church-membership-down -sharply-past-two-decades.aspx.

2. "Fast Facts about American Religion," Hartford Institute for Religion Research, http://hirr.hartsem.edu/research/fastfacts/fast_facts.html.

3. "Size of Congregation," ARDA, 2012, www.thearda.com/ConQS/qs_295.asp.

4. Queen, "I Want It All," by Brian May, track 4 on *The Miracle*, Capitol Records, 1989.

5. Quoted in Joseph Coohill, "Albert Einstein: The Definition of Insanity Is Doing the Same Thing Over and Over and Expecting Different Results," Professor Buzzkill, May 29, 2017, https://professorbuzzkill.com/einstein-insanity-qnq.

6. Bill Gaultiere, "Pastor Stress Statistics," www.soulshepherding.org/pastors-under -stress.

7. Craig D. Lounsbrough, "What I've Learned—Just by Watching," Craig D. Lounsbrough, www.craiglpc.com/ive-learned-just-watching.

8. Bob Hamp, "The Problem Jesus Came to Solve," video, 32:19, November 8, 2011, https://vimeo.com/31799897.

9. Jerry C. Bostick, quoted in Jerry Woodfill, "Origin of Apollo 13 Quote: 'Failure Is Not an Option,'" Space Acts, www.spaceacts.com/notanoption.htm.

10. Barna Research Group, as quoted in Howard Culbertson, "When Americans Become Christian," Southern Nazarene University, http://home.snu.edu /~hculbert/ages.htm.

11. "3339. Metamorphoó," Bible Hub, https://biblehub.com/greek/3339.htm.

12. Haydn Shaw, *Generational IQ: Christianity Isn't Dying, Millennials Aren't the Problem, and the Future Is Bright* (Carol Stream, IL: Tyndale), 20.

13. "Meditate the Word," Tom Brown Ministries, August 16, 2014, https://tombrownministriesblog.wordpress.com/2014/08/16/meditate-the-word/.

14. Bob Hamp, "The Problem Jesus Came to Solve," video, 32:19, November 8, 2011, https://vimeo.com/31799897.

15. "Strong's G5048—Teleioō," Blue Letter Bible, www.blueletterbible.org/lang /lexicon/lexicon.cfm?Strongs=G5048&t=KJV.

16. "Strong's G5281—Hypomonē," Blue Letter Bible, www.blueletterbible.org /lang/lexicon/lexicon.cfm?Strongs=G5281&t=KJV.

17. Lance Witt, *Replenish: Leading from a Healthy Soul* (Grand Rapids, MI: Baker Books, 2011), 208.

18. Witt, *Replenish*, 208.

19. Think Differently, https://tdcounseling.com.

20. Tony Morgan, *The Unstuck Church: Equipping Churches to Experience Sustained Health* (Nashville: Thomas Nelson, 2017), 2.

EQUIPPING LEADERS.
EQUIPPING THE CHURCH.

VISIONBOX

VisionBox Strategic Planning Kit: 5 Core Actions for a Healthy Small Church is a simple, team-based resource designed to help churches clarify five foundations of ministry by providing practical teaching, promoting focused discussion, and pushing leadership strategically forward.

95Network is a national non-profit organization that exists to resource the 95 percent of churches in the United States that are under 500 in average attendance. They do this through practical content, conferences, and grant funds for coaching and consulting. Since its inception, 95Network has helped hundreds of churches focus on creating a long-lasting and healthy ministry. Learn more at 95network.org.

Available from David C Cook or your Christian Retailer

DAVID C COOK

transforming lives together

At David C Cook, we equip the local church around
the corner and around the globe to make disciples.
Come see how we are working together—go to
www.davidccook.org. Thank you!

transforming lives together